At Issue

Gay and Lesbian Families

Other Books in the At Issue Series:

At Issue

Gay and Lesbian Families

Roman Espejo, Book Editor

GREENHAVEN PRESS
A part of Gale, Cengage Learning

GALE
CENGAGE Learning

Detroit • New York • San Francisco • New Haven, Conn • Waterville, Maine • London

Christine Nasso, *Publisher*
Elizabeth Des Chenes, *Managing Editor*

© 2009 Greenhaven Press, a part of Gale, Cengage Learning.

Gale and Greenhaven Press are registered trademarks used herein under license.

For more information, contact:
Greenhaven Press
27500 Drake Rd.
Farmington Hills, MI 48331-3535
Or you can visit our Internet site at gale.cengage.com

Articles in Greenhaven Press anthologies are often edited for length to meet page requirements. In addition, original titles of these works are changed to clearly present the main thesis and to explicitly indicate the author's opinion. Every effort is made to ensure that Greenhaven Press accurately reflects the original intent of the authors. Every effort has been made to trace the owners of copyrighted material.

Cover image © Images.com/Corbis.

LIBRARY OF CONGRESS CATALOGING-IN-PUBLICATION DATA

Gay and lesbian families / Roman Espejo, book editor.
    p. cm. -- (At issue)
  Includes bibliographical references and index.
  ISBN 978-0-7377-4302-9 (hardcover)
  ISBN 978-0-7377-4301-2 (pbk.)
  1. Same-sex marriage--United States. 2. Gay couples--Family relationships--United States. 3. Gays--Family relationships--United States. I. Espejo, Roman, 1977-
  HQ76.35.U6G396 2009
  306.84'8--dc22
                                                                    2009004708

Printed in the United States of America
1 2 3 4 5 6 7 13 12 11 10 09

Contents

Introduction

On May 15, 2008, the California Supreme Court annulled a same-sex marriage ban, and the ruling went into effect the following month. On November 4 of that year, voters in California narrowly passed Proposition 8, an initiative that amended the state's constitution to eliminate gay and lesbian couples' right to marry. According to a study conducted by the University of California, Los Angeles, an estimated 18,000 gay and lesbian couples wedded during this roughly six-month period. However, as of December 2008, the validity of these marriages may be in limbo, despite assurance from the state's attorney general, Jerry Brown. Shortly after the election results were announced, the Yes on 8 campaign said in an official statement that "only marriage between a man and a woman will be valid or recognized in California, regardless of when or where performed." And although the election results had not yet been certified the next day, many counties in California—among them San Francisco, Los Angeles, and San Diego—ceased issuing marriage licenses to gay and lesbian couples.

The battle for gays' and lesbians' rights to marry in California embodies the contemporary and polarized views of homosexuality, marriage, and family in America. For proponents of Proposition 8, voter approval was a victory on several key grounds. With the legalization of same-sex marriage, they maintain that under the California Education Code, public schools would have been required to teach students in sexual health classes that same-sex marriage is equal to heterosexual marriage—even if parents are unaware of this curriculum or object to it. In response to voter turnout on the proposition, Jennifer Roback Morse, founder and president of the Ruth Institute, declares, "The people of California are deeply troubled by the idea of small children being taught about homosexuality in the schools without their parents' knowledge or con-

sent." Others believe that Proposition 8 shields religious freedom and prevents values that do not condone homosexuality
from being marginalized even further. For example, in August
2008, the California Supreme Court ruled that sexual discrimination laws outweighed the religious rights of two Christian fertility doctors who refused to artificially inseminate a
lesbian. Finally, supporters insist that civil unions already
grant same-sex couples legal and financial benefits, and Proposition 8 upholds the traditional ideal of marriage and the
family. Ron Prentice, chairman of the Yes on 8 campaign,
maintains that the initiative "has always been about restoring
the traditional definition of marriage ... Gay and lesbian domestic partnerships will continue to enjoy the same legal
rights as married spouses." This definition is vital, advocates
of traditional marriage contend, because the institution of
marriage is a fundamental building block of society that would
deteriorate if redefined. President of the Institute of American
Values David Blankenhorn argues,

> The deep logic of same-sex marriage is clearly consistent
> with what scholars call deinstitutionalization—the overturn-
> ing or weakening of all of the customary forms of marriage,
> and the dramatic shrinking of marriage's public meaning
> and institutional authority. Does deinstitutionalization nec-
> essarily require gay marriage? Apparently not. For decades
> heterosexuals have been doing a fine job on that front all by
> themselves. But gay marriage clearly presupposes and rein-
> forces deinstitutionalization.

However, opponents to Proposition 8 staunchly counter
these assertions. First, they claim that the proposition's language did not include anything about public schools or education and that same-sex marriage will not enter curriculums
as a requirement. According to the campaign No on 8's Web
site, "California gives parents an absolute right to remove their
kids and opt-out of teaching on health and family instruction
they don't agree with." Detractors also allege that because the

campaign in favor of Proposition 8 was financially supported and spearheaded mainly by the Mormon church, the passage of Proposition 8 is an erosion of the separation between church and state, forcing religious views into California's constitution. In an opinion piece in the University of Wisconsin, Madison's student newspaper, Tom Hart, a senior political science major, maintain[s] that opposition to same-sex marriage is fronted by a religious minority, writing, "How could a country that prides itself in the inalienability of basic human rights turn a resounding blind eye to the rights of a large segment of its population?" Most importantly, critics of Proposition 8 argue that the legalization of same-sex marriage does not weaken but instead strengthens the institution of marriage by including and protecting diverse families. Before voters approved the initiative, Kate Kendall, executive director of the National Center for Lesbian Rights, proclaimed,

> The fundamental right that has been extended to same-sex couples to marry is not about severing the recognition of the importance of marriage to the stability of a family. It's about recognizing and expanding that to include same-sex couples who form relationships, who become economically interdependent, many of [whom] have children, live in neighborhoods, and who support their community, and who now finally in the state of California are supported and recognized as having their relationship recorded under civil law [with] the same dignity, respect, and security as anyone else.

Although it passed, Proposition 8 did not bring the same-sex marriage issue in California, let alone the rest of the nation, to a close. Three lawsuits against the proposition were filed on November 5, 2008, which were accepted by the California Supreme Court two weeks later, on the main premise that Proposition 8 revised—not amended—the state's constitution, rendering it invalid. In addition, the state of Massachusetts still recognizes these unions, and on October 10,

2008, the Connecticut Supreme Court ruled in favor of gays' and lesbians' right to marry, which became effective on November 12 of that year. In *At Issue: Gay and Lesbian Families*, the authors debate same-sex marriage and how homosexuality should be framed within the definition of family.

1

Gay Marriage Threatens Families, Children, and Society

Robert Benne and Gerald McDermott

Robert Benne is the Jordan-Trexler professor of religion and director of the Center for Religion and Society at Roanoke College in Salem, Virginia, where Gerald McDermott is a professor of religion.

As U.S. states legalize gay marriage, the negative effects of this new social trend must be examined. First, it would scramble the definition of marriage, undermining monogamy and opening the door to polygamous marriage. Second, gay marriage would harm children; those raised by gay and lesbian parents suffer high rates of suicide, depression, drug abuse, molestation within the family, and confusion about their sexual orientation. Third, legalization of gay marriage would have repercussions on a society already burdened with instability in marriage and family life and divided by abortion activism. Domestic partnerships can provide legal entitlements to same-sex couples, but the traditional definition of marriage must be upheld.

Now that the Massachusetts Supreme Court has ruled that marriage must be open to gays and lesbians, it is time to consider the question that pops up more than mushrooms after a spring rain: How would the legalization of gay marriage harm current and future heterosexual marriages?

The answer at first glance is that it wouldn't, at least not in individual cases in the short run. But what about the longer run for everyone?

It is a superficial kind of individualism that does not recognize the power of emerging social trends that often start with only a few individuals bucking conventional patterns of behavior. Negative social trends start with only a few aberrations. Gradually, however, social sanctions weaken and individual aberrations became a torrent.

Think back to the 1960s, when illegitimacy and cohabitation were relatively rare. At that time, many asked how one young woman having a baby out of wedlock or living with an unmarried man could hurt their neighbors. Now we know the negative social effects these two living arrangements have spawned: lower marriage rates, more instability in the marriages that are enacted, more fatherless children, increased rates of domestic violence and poverty, and a vast expansion of welfare state expenses.

But even so, why would a new social trend of gays marrying have negative effects? We believe there are compelling reasons why the institutionalization of gay marriage would be 1) bad for marriage, 2) bad for children, and 3) bad for society.

Bad for Marriage

1. The first casualty of the acceptance of gay marriage would be the very definition of marriage itself. For thousands of years and in every Western society, marriage has meant the life-long union of a man and a woman. Such a statement about marriage is what philosophers call an analytic proposition. The concept of marriage necessarily includes the idea of a man and woman committing themselves to each other. Any other arrangement contradicts the basic definition. Advocates of gay marriage recognize this contradiction by proposing "gay unions" instead, but this distinction is, we believe, a strategic one. The ultimate goal for them is the societal acceptance of gay marriage.

Scrambling the definition of marriage will be a shock to our fundamental understanding of human social relations and institutions. One effect will be that sexual fidelity will be detached from the commitment of marriage. The advocates of gay marriage themselves admit as much. "Among gay male relationships, the openness of the contract makes it more likely to survive than many heterosexual bonds," Andrew Sullivan, the most eloquent proponent of gay marriage, wrote in his 1996 book, *Virtually Normal.* "There is more likely to be a greater understanding of the need for extramarital outlets between two men than between a man and a woman. . . . Something of the gay relationship's necessary honesty, its flexibility, and its equality could undoubtedly help strengthen and inform many heterosexual bonds."

In short, gay marriage will change marriage more than it will change gays.

The former moderator of the Metropolitan Community Church, a largely homosexual denomination, made the same point. "Monogamy is not a word the gay community uses," Troy Perry told *The Dallas Morning News* "We talk about fidelity. That means you live in a loving, caring, honest relationship with your partner. Because we can't marry, we have people with widely varying opinions as to what that means. Some would say that committed couples could have multiple sexual partners as long as there's no deception."

A recent study from the Netherlands, where gay marriage is legal, suggests that the moderator is correct. Researchers found that even among stable homosexual partnerships, men have an average of eight partners per year outside their "monogamous" relationship.

In short, gay marriage will change marriage more than it will change gays.

Further, if we scramble our definition of marriage, it will soon embrace relationships that will involve more than two persons. Prominent advocates hope to use gay marriage as a wedge to abolish governmental support for traditional marriage altogether. Law Professor Martha Ertman of the University of Utah, for example, wants to render the distinction between traditional marriage and "polyamory" (group marriage) "morally neutral." She argues that greater openness to gay partnerships will help us establish this moral neutrality. (Her main article on this topic, in the Winter 2001 *Harvard Civil Rights and Civil Liberties Law Review*, is not available online, but she made a similar case in the Spring/Summer 2001 *Duke Journal Of Gender Law & Policy*.) University of Michigan law professor David Chambers wrote in a widely cited 1996 *Michigan Law Review* piece that he expects gay marriage will lead government to be "more receptive to [marital] units of three or more."

Bad for Children

2. Gay marriage would be bad for children. According to a recent article in *Child Trends*, "Research clearly demonstrates that family structure matters for children, and the family structure that helps the most is a family headed by two biological parents in a low-conflict marriage." While gay marriage would encourage adoption of children by homosexual couples, which may be preferable to foster care, some lesbian couples want to have children through anonymous sperm donations, which means some children will be created purposely without knowledge of one of their biological parents. Research has also shown that children raised by homosexuals are more dissatisfied with their own gender, suffer a greater rate of molestation within the family, and have homosexual experiences more often.

Gay marriage will also encourage teens who are unsure of their sexuality to embrace a lifestyle that suffers high rates of suicide, depression, HIV, drug abuse, STDs, and other pathogens. This is particularly alarming because, according to a 1991 scientific survey among 12-year-old boys, more than 25 percent feel uncertain about their sexual orientations. We have already seen that lesbianism is "chic" in certain elite social sectors.

Finally, acceptance of gay marriage will strengthen the notion that marriage is primarily about adult yearnings for intimacy and is not essentially connected to raising children. Children will be hurt by those who will too easily bail out of a marriage because it is not "fulfilling" to them.

Bad for Society

3. Gay marriage would be bad for society. The effects we have described above will have strong repercussions on a society that is already having trouble maintaining wholesome stability in marriage and family life. If marriage and families are the foundation for a healthy society, introducing more uncertainty and instability in them will be bad for society.

In addition, we believe that gay marriage can only be imposed by activist judges, not by the democratic will of the people. The vast majority of people define marriage as the life-long union of a man and a woman. They will strongly resist redefinition. Like the 1973 judicial activism regarding abortion, the imposition of gay marriage would bring contempt for the law and our courts in the eyes of many Americans. It would exacerbate social conflict and division in our nation, a division that is already bitter and possibly dangerous.

In summary, we believe that the introduction of gay marriage will seriously harm Americans—including those in heterosexual marriages—over the long run. Strong political measures may be necessary to maintain the traditional definition of marriage, possibly even a constitutional amendment.

Some legal entitlements sought by gays and lesbians might be addressed by recognizing non-sexually defined domestic partnerships. But as for marriage, let us keep the definition as it is, and strengthen our capacity to live up to its ideals.

2

Gay Parenting Places Children at Risk

Real Women of Canada's REALity Magazine

Founded in 1983, REAL (Realistic, Equal, Active, for Life) Women of Canada is a nonpartisan and nondemoninational advocacy group for traditional values.

The studies that homosexual lobbies use to bolster their claims that gay parenting is equal to heterosexual parenting are deeply flawed and should not shape politics or government. On the contrary, research and analyses conclude that gay parenting is detrimental to children on numerous accounts, resulting in higher incidences of mental health problems and homosexual behavior as well as greater exposure to parental violence and sexual abuse. Statements from the scientific community that promote gay parenting have much more to do with politics and pressure from homosexual activists than valid social science.

The Canadian Psychological Association has ceased to be a scientific organization and instead has become a political organization promoting politically correct thought.

In November 2003, the Association made the startling announcement that there is no heightened risk of problems from same-sex parenting, or an increased likelihood for children living in such partnerships to become gay themselves.

According to the Association, "studies have shown almost no difference in sexual preference or in psychosocial development for children of same-sex parents." On what basis did the Association reach such a conclusion? Certainly, it could not have looked at recent findings in social science journals to reach this conclusion. If the Association had troubled itself to look at the current literature, it would have, in all decency, been disturbed by their conclusions, and, with professional integrity, issued quite a different statement.

According to the *American Journal of Diseases of Children* and *The Advocate*, close to 60% of adolescent AIDS sufferers were infected by adult bisexual and homosexual men. Thousands of these American boys are now dead. The same is probably true for other western countries like Canada, where many young runaway boys end up prostituting themselves for men.

Child development is fragile and a complicated matter. Several million years of heterosexuality explain the present human condition. A family headed by two men or two women is a new phenomenon, which entails great uncertainty.

It is bizarre, therefore, that experts and politicians often express concerns about the emotional impact of single-parent families on children, as indicated by the Statistics Canada National Longitudinal Survey of Children and Youth, October, 1996, while, on the other hand, they appear to be absolutely indifferent to the plight of children who grow up in same-sex partnership arrangements. Public policy makers should be concerned—deeply concerned.

Same-Sex Parenting

According to the recent quantitative analysis on same-sex parenting by [researchers Robert] Lerner and [Althea K.] Nagai, 49 American studies, which advocate homosexual parenting, have fatal flaws, rendering them statistically invalid (non-representative samples, imprecise hypotheses, confused political objectives, etc.). The researchers concluded that the studies repeatedly referred to by American, European and Canadian homosexual lobbies should not be used to influence the politics of their respective governments. This conclusion was also expressed by ... Stephen L. Nock, Professor of Sociology, University of Virginia, who, in an affidavit submitted by the federal Attorney General in the Ontario Court of Appeal same-sex marriage case, evaluated statistics on same-sex parenting and concluded that the studies were flawed in either design or execution, which rendered them totally invalid.

According to a paper published by Professor Bradley P. Hayton, there are serious concerns about the effects of a homosexual lifestyle on children.

Other studies have also reported that boys raised by homosexual mothers may have a lower self-image, regarding masculinity.

Professor Hayton states:

Homosexuals ... model a poor view of marriage to children. They are taught by example and belief that marital relationships are transitory and most sexual in nature. Sexual relationships are primarily for pleasure rather than procreation. And they are taught that monogamy in a marriage is not the norm [and] should be discouraged if one wants a good 'marital' relationship.

The reason that same-sex parenting is detrimental to the well being of children is due to several factors:

1. Higher Incidence of Violence.

There is a higher rate of violence in lesbian and homosexual relationships than in married, heterosexual relationships. A study in the *Journal of Interpersonal Violence* examined conflict and violence in lesbian relationships. The researchers found that 90% of the lesbians surveyed had been recipients of one or more acts of verbal aggression from their intimate partners during the year prior to this study, with 31% reporting one or more incidents of physical abuse. This is verified in a number of other studies. According to the homosexual authors of *Men Who Beat the Men Who Love Them*, domestic violence affects half of all gay couples. The vast majority of violent crimes against homosexuals are committed by homosexuals, and are not considered hate crimes. According to the leading U.S. gay magazine *The Advocate*, 75% of its readers admit engaging in violent sex, 20% in sadistic sex, and 55% are using painful objects.

2. Higher Incidence of Mental Health Problem

There is a higher incidence of mental health problems among homosexuals and lesbians. These include problems of substance abuse, as well as a greater risk for suicide. Homophobia is often blamed for the high suicide rate of young gays, but this cause is only one among many, such as prostitution, broken families, sexual assault at a young age, disappointments in love affairs, and premature homosexual labeling.

3. Reduced Life Expectancy.

Male homosexuals have a significantly reduced life expectancy. A study published in the *International Journal of Epidemiology* on the mortality rates of homosexuals stated as follows:

In a major Canadian center, life expectancy at age twenty for gay and bisexual men is eight to twenty years less than for all men. If the same pattern of mortality were to continue, we estimate that nearly half of gay and bisexual men currently aged twenty years will not reach their sixty-fifth birthday. Under even the most liberal assumptions, gay and bisexual men in this urban center are now experiencing a life expectancy similar to that experienced by all men in Canada in the year 1871.

4. Higher Incidence of Same-Sex Orientation.

Same-sex parents are inclined to influence their children's sexual orientation. A study published in the *Archives of Sexual Behavior* stated as follows:

There are developmentally important, statistically significant differences between children reared by homosexual parents compared to heterosexual parents. For example, children raised by homosexuals were found to have greater parental encouragement for cross-gender behaviour [and] greater amounts of cross-dressing and cross-gender play/role behaviour.

5. Greater Risk of Sexual Involvement with Parents.

According to a study published in *Adolescence*, 29% of the adult children of homosexual parents have been specifically subjected to sexual molestation as a child by a homosexual parent, compared to only 0.6 percent of adult children of heterosexual parents.

These findings were confirmed in a study published in the *American Sociological Review*.

6. Greater Risk of Social or Psychological Problems.

The vast majority of the American studies widely used by homosexual activists claim that same-sex parenting is as valid as opposite-sex parenting. However, as mentioned previously, these earlier studies have been found to be seriously flawed. According to a study there were noticeable problems with children raised by same-sex parents in regard to discipline expectations, and general parent–child relationships. Other studies have also reported that boys raised by homosexual mothers may have a lower self-image regarding masculinity.

A study of children of lesbians revealed many problems, including a "defensiveness" on the part of the children of lesbian couples she studied, a pattern of denial—especially deep in the youngest child in the lesbian couples, hostility from older boys, especially directed at the mother's lesbian lover, the children expressed concern for the welfare of siblings, the children had concerns about their own sexuality, the children had concerns about the integrity of their family, concerns about their mother's homosexual activities, there was evidence that one of the lesbian mothers expressly encouraged her daughters to make lesbian sexual choices, and that the children were forced to conceal one parent's secret sexual behaviours from the other parent.

All these problems have led to the children raised by same-sex parents becoming dysfunctional and disadvantaged.

7. Higher Incidence of Child Molestation.

Proportionately, homosexual men are more inclined to child molestation than heterosexual men.

According to American studies, the evidence indicates that homosexual men molest boys and teenagers at rates completely disproportionate to the rates at which heterosexual men molest girls. A study shows that the homosexual child molester accounts for approximately 7 times more victims than the heterosexual molester. When it comes to child sex abuse, men are almost always the perpetrator. Less than 3% of the population is homosexual, yet one-third of the sex abuse cases are committed against boys.

Although pedophilia is condemned by most homosexuals, it remains condoned by many leading gay and lesbian

North American activists who lobby for the lowering of the age of consent for sex. Early sex is said to be healthy for boys, claims the self-proclaimed homosexual association NAMBLA (North American Man Boy Love Association). Intergenerational sex (an often used euphemism for pederasty), is an undeniable fixture of gay literature, gay films, gay travel and gay prostitution. In the 70s, *The Advocate* repeatedly ran full-page ads for a "penetrable boy doll," and in the 90s, 21% of its readers admitted having been molested before the age of 15.

Politics and Pressure

What is behind the statement by the Canadian Psychological Association? Are its members just plain mad? Clearly, its statement on same-sex parenting has a lot to do with politics and pressure from homosexual activists. Unfortunately, the Association's conclusions have almost nothing to do with genuine social science research. The Canadian Psychological Association should be embarrassed and ashamed.

3

Gay Parenting Does Not Place Children at Risk

Leslie Cooper, Paul Cates, and Judith Stacey

Leslie Cooper is a senior staff attorney for the Lesbian and Gay Rights Project at the American Civil Liberties Union, a national organization that works to defend civil rights guaranteed by the U.S. Constitution. Paul Cates is the public education director for the project. Judith Stacey is a sociology professor at New York University and a senior scholar with the Council on Contemporary Families.

The body of social science does not give credence to the claims that gays and lesbians are inferior to heterosexuals as parents and that such parenting harms children. Research asserting that children raised by married heterosexual couples are less likely to engage in at-risk behavior compares them to single heterosexual mothers and fathers, not homosexual parents. Furthermore, conservative activists skew these findings: It is the lack of two parents to provide guidance and resources—not the absence of a mother and father—that adversely affects children. The differences that studies do demonstrate, such as the tendency of children raised in gay households to conform less to gender roles and, if they occur, show greater acceptance of same-sex attractions, have also been misrepresented by conservative activists and journalists.

Leslie Cooper, Paul Cates, and Judith Stacey, "Chapter 4: The Social Science: A Conversation with Judith Stacey," *Too High a Price: The Case Against Restricting Gay Parenting*, Updated Second Edition, New York, NY: American Civil Liberties Union Foundation, 2006, pp. 34–38. Copyright © 2006 American Civil Liberties Union. Reprinted with permission of the American Civil Liberties Union, www.aclu.org.

Judith Stacey is a professor of sociology at New York University and a senior scholar with the Council on Contemporary Families. In 2001, she and Timothy J. Biblarz published a review of the social science research on lesbian and gay parenting, "(How) Does the Sexual Orientation of Parents Matter?" in the *American Sociological Review*.

Conservative activists everywhere argue that heterosexuals make better parents than gay men and lesbians. Is there anything in the body of social science research that supports this claim?

No, nothing at all. Significant, reliable social scientific evidence indicates that lesbian and gay parents are at least as fit, effective, and successful as heterosexual parents. The research also shows that children of same-sex couples are as emotionally healthy and socially adjusted and at least as educationally and socially successful as children raised by heterosexual parents. No credible social science evidence supports a claim to the contrary.

What about all the research showing that children raised by married couples are much less likely to have a host of problems such as juvenile delinquency, involvement with drugs, dropping out of school, and teen pregnancy?

The body of research you're referring to compares children raised by single and married couple heterosexual parents. Lesbian and gay parents and their children are not included in this research. All of the research that compares children based on their parents' sexual orientation finds that this factor has no impact on their healthy development.

Conservative activists are misrepresenting the single-parenthood research as showing that children need a mother and a father—a male and a female parent—and, thus, that gay couples are poorer parents. That is simply not true. The research shows that the poorer outcomes for children in single-parent families are not attributable to the gender of the parents. They are consequences of having one parent instead of two to supervise, guide, and provide resources for a child, and the unfortunate byproducts of divorce for many children such as conflict, the loss of a relationship with one parent, and dislocations such as moving to a new neighborhood and changing schools. The leading scholars on single-parent families agree that the absence of a male or female parent is not the issue for these children; it's the absence of a second parent and the negative circumstances that often accompany divorce. There is no evidence that the gender combination of parents represents a risk factor for healthy child development.

A Double Standard

Some opponents of lesbian and gay parenthood argue that the studies you cite . . . are not reliable because they used flawed research methods and resulted in flawed findings. What is your response?

The studies that have been conducted are certainly not perfect—virtually no study is. First, it's almost never possible to transform complex social relationships, such as parent–child relationships, into distinct and meaningful quantifiable measures. Second, because many lesbians and gay men remain in the closet, we cannot know if the participants in the studies are representative of all gay people. However, the studies we reviewed are just as reliable and respected as studies in most other areas of child development and psychology. They generally compare well-matched groups of children with heterosexual and lesbian or gay parents. The studies we discussed have been published in rigorously peer-reviewed and highly selective journals, whose standards represent expert consensus on generally accepted social scientific standards for research on child development. Those journals include *Child Development* and *Developmental Psychology*, the two flagship journals in the field of child development. The first is published by the

5,000-member academic Society for Research in Child Development, and the second is published by the American Psychological Association.

We were unable to find a single social scientist conducting and publishing research in the area of children's development who claims to have found that gay and lesbian parents harm children.

So those critics of this body of research are really leveling attacks on well-accepted social science methods. Yet, they do not raise objections to studies that are even less rigorous or generalizable on such issues as the impact of divorce on children. It seems evident that the critics employ a double standard. They attack these particular studies not because the research methods differ from, or are inferior to, most studies of family relationships, but because these critics politically oppose equal family rights for lesbians and gay men.

There are other articles out there that not only criticize the studies you cite but also come up with findings that actually say lesbians and gay men should not be parents. Why don't you include those studies in your review?

We were unable to find a single social scientist conducting and publishing research in the area of children's development who claims to have found that gay and lesbian parents harm children. The only legitimate disagreement among scholars concerns the degree of confidence they place in the generalizability of the existing research to all lesbians and gay men.

When people claim that there are studies showing that gay parents harm children, most often they are referring to the work of Paul Cameron. Paul Cameron has been completely discredited as a social scientist. He was dropped from membership in the American Psychological Association and censured by the American Sociological Association for unethical scholarly practices, such as misrepresenting research.

Rarely is there as much consensus in any area of social science as in the case of gay parenting, which is why the American Academy of Pediatrics and all of the major professional organizations with expertise in child welfare have issued reports and resolutions in support of gay and lesbian parental rights.

Misrepresenting the Differences

A few years ago, you and your colleague Tim Biblarz released a review of the then existing studies on lesbian and gay parenting. This review caused a bit of a commotion in the media. Are people representing the review accurately? What did you say in the review that caused so much controversy?

In our review we found that many researchers in this field shied away from studying or analyzing any areas of difference between families with lesbian and gay parents and those with heterosexual parents. In contrast, we emphasized some of the scattered findings of small but interesting differences that have been reported in some of this research, particularly in the areas of gender and sexual conformity. Conservative activists and journalists immediately seized on our discussion of these differences and began to cite these and our article as evidence in support of their efforts to deny partnership and parenting rights to lesbians and gay men. This is a serious misreading and abuse of our work. None of the differences reported in the research apply to child self-esteem, psychological well-being, or social adjustment. Nor were there differences in parents' self-esteem, mental health, or commitment to their children. In other words, even though we noted some differences, we emphasized that the differences were not deficits. In fact, the studies found no negative effects of lesbian and gay parenting, and a few studies reported some differences that could represent a few advantages of lesbian parenting.

What are some of the differences you noted?

Well, for example, several studies find that lesbian co-mothers share family responsibilities more equally than heterosexual married parents, and some research hints that children benefit from egalitarian co-parenting.

A few studies found that lesbians worry less than heterosexual parents about the gender conformity of their children. Perhaps that helps to account for a few studies that found that sons of lesbians play less aggressively and that children of lesbians communicate their feelings more freely, aspire to a wider range of occupations, and score higher on self-esteem. I think most people would see these as positive things, but some of the critics have misrepresented these differences as evidence that the children are suffering from gender confusion.

Finally, some studies reported that lesbian mothers feel more comfortable discussing sexuality with their children and accepting their children's sexuality, whatever it might be. More to the point are data reported in a 15-year British study. Although few of the young adults identified themselves as gay or lesbian, a larger minority of those with lesbian mothers did report that they had at one time or another considered or actually had engaged in a same-sex relationship.

Far More Complicated

Are you saying that the social science finds that children of lesbians and gay men are more likely to be gay themselves?

Sexuality is far more complicated than that. Most gay adults, after all, were brought up by straight parents. We are still in the dark ages when it comes to understanding the roots of specific sexual attractions. Regardless of the relative impact of nature and nurture, it seems likely that growing up with gay parents should reduce a child's reluctance to acknowledge, accept, or act upon same-sex sexual desires if they experience them. Because the first generation of children parented by self-identified lesbians or gay men are only now reaching adulthood, it is too soon to know if the finding in that one study will prove to be generally true. Personally, I would not be surprised to find that to be the case.

In 2004, a federal appeals court upheld the Florida law banning adoption by lesbians and gay men. In its opinion, the court cited the Stacey and Biblarz article as saying that the body of research on children of gay parents is methodologically flawed and that children raised by gay parents fare worse on some measures. Did you say that?

That's almost exactly the opposite of what we said. We are aware that conservative activist groups are misrepresenting our work in their efforts to restrict parenting by lesbians and gay men, but it is especially disturbing to see a court mischaracterize what we said.

Our paper discussed a number of the challenges faced by those researching children of gay parents, including the difficulty of drawing a random, representative sample of this population given that the complicated and diverse meanings of *gay* mean that we can't even know how many gay people there are, and some gay parents might be reluctant to come out because of persistent homophobia. We did not characterize the research as flawed or otherwise suggest that it is not solid, reliable research. In fact, we made it very clear that we sharply disagree with the conservative activists' characterization of the quality of this body of research. There are numerous studies that meet the high standards of the field. By now we have quite robust findings that there is absolutely no reason to be concerned that children of gay parents will be harmed or experience any problems in adjustment. In our review, we concluded:

> Because every relevant study to date shows that parental sexual orientation per se has no measurable effect on the quality of parent child relationships or on children's mental health or social adjustment, there is no evidentiary basis for considering parental sexual orientation in decisions about children's "best interest."

Has there been any new research on children of lesbian and gay parents since the Stacey and Biblarz review article was published?

Since our 2001 article, many new studies have appeared on planned lesbian parenthood, generally couples who had children through donor insemination. We also now have some research with representative national or community samples. And new research on planned gay fatherhood through adoption or surrogacy is under way.

Are there any parental factors that have been shown to negatively impact children?

Some factors in parents have been found consistently to correlate with problems in child development. These include poverty, a low level of parental education, a high level of conflict between parents, and depression in parents. On the other hand, "authoritative" (rather than authoritarian) parenting by emotionally responsive, reliable, and consistent adults generally correlates with positive child outcomes.

4

Gay Adoption Should Be Accepted

Julian Sanchez

Julian Sanchez is a contributing editor for Reason, *a libertarian monthly magazine.*

Barriers to gay adoption deprive children of loving, stable families. Youngsters (often with special needs) in foster care pass through home after home instead of being placed permanently in, or are uprooted from, nurturing gay households. Additionally, blocks to second-parent adoption for gay and lesbian couples deprive their children of having two guardians with full legal authority. These legal obstacles, however, are clearly unwarranted: Opponents' charges that gay parenting is harmful and increases the risk of sexual abuse are rejected by social scientists. In fact, the children of gay and lesbian couples would say that homophobia and the burgeoning assault on gay parenting pose the real threat.

Wayne LaRue Smith had never been so happy to be called *bitch.*

About two months earlier, Smith and his partner, Dan Skahen, had taken in a 3-year-old foster child we'll call Charlie. The boy had emerged from the caseworker's car redolent of stale cigarette smoke, hair matted and tangled, barely able to walk, and, except for the occasional raspy cry, stone silent. "We think," whispered the caseworker, leaning in, "he's retarded."

Week after week, Smith recalls, Charlie refused to say anything. Then one day, as Smith was trying to prevent the boy from climbing around on the furniture, Charlie uttered the first word Smith had heard escape his lips: "Bitch!" Nonplussed at the vocabulary ("He didn't learn that language from us!" Smith says), Smith was nevertheless delighted that the child had said *something*. His silence broken, Charlie pressed his tiny fists to his hips and added "Asshole!" before scampering away. Within weeks he was speaking in complete—and more polite—sentences.

Charlie wasn't retarded. He had simply withdrawn from a world that until then hadn't given him much reason to be engaged with it. That sort of history, sadly, is shared by many of the children who find their way into the nation's foster care systems, which included half a million kids when the [U.S.] Department of Health and Human Services last counted, with some 126,000 available for adoption. At the end of fiscal year 2003, 30,000 of those children were in Florida, more than in any other state except New York and California, with more than 5,000 available for adoption.

Charlie lucked out with Skahen and Smith. As of [April 2004], Florida could not even account for the whereabouts of more than 500 children nominally in its custody. Every few years, the state's papers dutifully report an especially tragic case of a child rescued from a bad home only to be deposited by the state into some fresh hell. One such child is Yusimil Herrera, who, after being moved dozens of times from one foster home to another, homes in which she was beaten and sexually abused, won a famous lawsuit against the state in 1999. (The verdict was later overturned, and Herrera settled her claim.) She now stands accused of murdering her own young daughter.

Charlie was one of 23 foster children Skahen and Smith have taken in since 1999. The two boys they're now looking after have been with them for years, and Smith and Skahen would like to adopt them, to spare them the prospect of who-knows-how-many desultory transitions from foster family to foster family.

But in Florida, thanks to orange juice pitchwoman Anita Bryant's 1977 "Save the Children" campaign, the Department of Children and Families' adoption forms carry a pair of "yes" and "no" check boxes—page 5, part II, section G—below the statements "I am a homosexual" and "I am a bisexual." Check "yes" to either and you're ineligible to adopt. The law, as its sponsor explained shortly after it passed, was meant to alert gays that "we wish you'd go back into the closet."

The human desire for family isn't exclusive to hetero-sexuals, and attempts to prevent gays from raising families both stigmatize them and threaten to deprive them of an important component of a full life.

Thanks to this law, Skahen and Smith can log on to the Department of Children and Families' Web site and find a photograph and description of their older boy, on offer to any nice heterosexual couple who'd like to take him away from his family.

Right now only Florida explicitly prohibits any gay person from adopting, but just [ten] states and the District of Columbia explicitly *allow* adoptions by homosexuals. In most cases there's no formal policy, and several states either are known for family judges disinclined to grant homosexuals custody or have indirect statutory barriers to gay parenting. Nebraska banned gay foster parenting in 1995. Mississippi and Utah allow only married couples to adopt, a restriction geared in both cases to exclude gay couples. Just under half of U.S. states permit "second-parent adoption," which grants parental rights to both members of an unmarried couple, in at least some jurisdictions. And more restrictions may be on the way.

From a civil libertarian perspective, it's clear enough why the unequal treatment of gay parents is objectionable: The human desire for family isn't exclusive to heterosexuals, and attempts to prevent gays from raising families both stigmatize them and threaten to deprive them of an important component of a full life. But these barriers to adoption should also offend anyone concerned about family values—about ensuring that all children, especially those who have suffered in the past, find loving homes, and that enrolling those kids in school or getting them medical care is a simple, routine procedure, not a legalistic obstacle course. Yet "family values" remains the call to arms of many who support restricted parenting.

Better an Orphanage?

In 2004 the U.S. Supreme Court refused to hear an appeal of a lower court decision upholding Florida's ban on gay adoption. The challenge was brought by the American Civil Liberties Union on behalf of Smith, Skahen, and other gay parents. Among the plaintiffs were Steve Lofton and Roger Croteau, who care for five children born with HIV. Three of the kids have been with the couple since infancy.

"Good," reacted *World* Editor Marvin Olasky on the Christian news magazine's weblog. "Maybe more states will now pass legislation protecting kids from gay adoption." Mathew D. Staver, head of Liberty Counsel, which filed an amicus brief supporting Florida's policy, agreed. "Children in Florida will be benefited," he opined to the Christian news service AgapePress, "but not only that—I think other states will follow Florida's lead to enact similar laws."

Some lawmakers and judges in other states do indeed share a horror of gay parenthood. In 2003, as he introduced a bill to ban gay foster parenting, Texas legislator Robert Talton (R-Pasadena) told the state's House of Representatives: "If it was me I would rather [leave] kids in orphanages as such— this is where they are now if they're not fostered out. At least they have a chance of learning the proper values." (Texas doesn't actually have orphanages, but you get the point.) Talton pushed a similar bill through his state's House in April [2005] though Talton's language was later stripped from the Senate version of the law. Former Alabama Supreme Court Judge Roy Moore used uncommonly vehement language, but perhaps not uncommon logic, when he wrote in 2000 that a lesbian mother should be denied custody of her three children because homosexuality was "an evil disfavored under the law," and that the state should "use its power to prevent the subversion of children toward this lifestyle, to not encourage a criminal lifestyle."

As the ranks of gay parents swell, they become more visible—and more visible targets.

State legislatures are now pushing to erect a variety of legal barriers to gay couples seeking to raise kids. Carrie Evans, state legislative lawyer for the Human Rights Campaign, a gay advocacy group, has tracked state legislation on gay parenting since 2000. "This year [2005] has been the worst," says Evans. "Usually we have a few, but I've never seen this many in one year." Just four months into 2005, lawmakers in seven states— Alabama, Arkansas, Indiana, Oregon, Tennessee, Texas, and Virginia—had introduced bills that would restrict the parenting rights of gay couples and individuals. This new assault seems to be the result of several complementary factors:

The Gay Baby Boom: Extrapolating from 2000 census data, Urban Institute demographer Gary Gates conservatively estimates there are at least a quarter million children living in households headed by same-sex couples; 4.2 percent are either adopted or foster children, almost double the figure for heterosexual couples. (Single gay parents, of course, are not captured by those numbers.) While the increase in gay parenting can't be precisely measured, Gates estimates that one in 20 male same-sex couples and one in five female couples were raising children in 1990. By 2000 those figures had risen to one in five for male couples and one in three for female couples. A 2003 survey by the Evan B. Donaldson Adoption Institute found that 60 percent of adoption agencies place children in gay households, and a 2001 Kaiser Family Foundation survey found that, while about 8 percent of gay respondents were currently parents or guardians of children under 18, almost half of those who weren't hoped to one day adopt children of their own. As the ranks of gay parents swell, they become more visible—and more visible targets.

The Tipping Point: A 2004 Harris poll found that a plurality of Americans still disapproves of adoption by same-sex couples—43 percent and 45 percent for female and male couples, respectively. But that represents a dramatic decrease in opposition since 1996, when majorities of more than 60 percent disapproved in both cases. Conservatives may worry, with good reason, that if laws restricting gay parenting aren't locked in now, perhaps drawing strength from the momentum behind anti-gay marriage legislation, their time will soon have passed.

The Marriage Factor: "Among both the youngest and oldest cohorts," a 2003 study by the Pew Forum on Religion and Public Life found, "those who know someone who is gay are about twice as likely to favor gay marriage as those who do not." The expansion of gay parenting means people who might not otherwise encounter gay couples will be more likely to see them at PTA meetings and Little League games. And the Harris poll found an overwhelming majority agrees that children being raised by gay couples should "have the same rights as all other children." For practical purposes, that means ensuring that their parents have rights too. If, other things being equal, it's better for children to be raised by married couples, then as the number of kids raised by gays increases, the conservative case for expanding marriage rights becomes more potent. All of which means that as more same-sex couples raise children, opposition to gay marriage is likely to erode—a matter of concern to the social conservatives on whom Republican politicians increasingly rely for support.

The Lawrence *Effect:* Until recently, sodomy laws in 13 states confirmed Judge Moore's assessment of homosexuality as "an evil disfavored under the law." But in the 2003 case *Lawrence v. Texas,* the Supreme Court held that sodomy laws were unconstitutional, yielding, in the words of the Human Rights Campaign's Evans, "rapid changes in custody and visitation case law." The *Lawrence* decision, she explains, "really helped us because for a long time, especially in adoption cases, judges restricted gay parents' rights on the grounds that sodomy was a felony." But now the baton has been passed to lawmakers, who know that courts are more deferential to legislators on questions of family policy than on issues of sexual privacy.

"Kids Need a Mom and Dad": Even Americans otherwise favorably disposed to gay rights may have concerns about how growing up in a gay household affects children. Traditionalists have done their best to heighten those concerns, arguing that discriminatory laws serve the best interests of kids.

The Phantom Menace

The mantra that "children need a mother and a father" has acquired a patina of conventional wisdom through frequent repetition. Yet there is little evidence that children raised by gay couples fare worse than other children.

Gay rights opponents such as Family Research Institute chief Paul Cameron and the Family Research Council's Timothy Dailey are fond of arguing that gay men are disproportionately likely to molest children—a potent charge rejected by the serious social scientists who have directly investigated it. Large-scale studies of molestation victims have repeatedly found that abusers overwhelmingly were either heterosexual in adult relationships or lacked any sexual response to adults.

Noting that about a third of molestation cases involve male adults targeting male children, Dailey and Cameron insist those adults must, by definition, be homosexual. Since homosexual men make up a far smaller proportion of the general population, Dailey reasons, gay men must be disproportionately likely to abuse children.

The problem with this view is that psychologists generally regard pedophilia an orientation of its own. Men who molest boys are not necessarily—indeed, are almost never—"gay" in the colloquial sense. Even if one accepts a definition that calls such men "homosexual," the fact remains that there is little overlap between that group and men who pursue romantic relationships with other adult men, the relevant comparison group for gay adoption.

Most child welfare professionals don't see things Dailey and Cameron's way. After reviewing the available data in 2002, the American Academy of Pediatrics endorsed second-parent adoption rights for gay couples. A resolution passed by the American Psychological Association in 2004 declared that there was "no scientific evidence that parenting effectiveness is related to parental sexual orientation: lesbian and gay parents are as likely as heterosexual parents to provide supportive and healthy environments for their children." It also noted that "the children of lesbian and gay parents are as likely as those of heterosexual parents to flourish."

The Child Welfare League of America, an organization founded in 1920 that now comprises more than 1,100 public and private agencies providing child services, filed an amicus brief in 2004 supporting the ACLU's challenge to Florida's adoption ban, noting the consensus that "children are not adversely affected by their parents' lesbian or gay orientation" and that "all of the mainstream professional organizations in the fields of child health and welfare agree that there is no basis to exclude gay men and lesbians from adopting children." That same year, an Arkansas circuit court overturned a state Child Welfare Agency Review Board regulation prohibiting gay foster parenting after extensive fact finding, including testimony from a variety of psychologists, social workers, and sociologists, concluding that the ban contradicted the agency's mandate to serve the best interests of children.

The statistical evidence meshes with the experience of Adam Pertman, executive director of the Donaldson Institute, an adoption policy-research organization, and author of *Adoption Nation*. "The evidence on the ground, based on the markers that we have, is that these are good families," he says. "The social workers I talk to are asking how they can recruit more [gay parents], because they're working. That's the best validation I can think of, unless you think all these child welfare professionals are out to harm kids."

Even on the assumption that heterosexual households are somehow better for children, some restrictions on gay parenting are hard to fathom.

Opponents of gay parenting, for the most part, have been forced to fall back on the assertion that the jury's still out. Noting—correctly—that none of the research on children of gay couples made use of the large random samples that generate the most robust results, they claim studies to date provide no basis for supposing that gay parents won't be inferior. But as New York University sociologist Judith Stacey argues, "they have to stretch pretty far to find that. The studies have been very consistent and very positive." Stacey concedes that most of them are "small scale" but adds that "there are some 50 studies now, and we don't see them going the other way. I have yet to see one legitimate refereed publication or scholar come out with a generally negative finding."

As in so many other disputes, child welfare may be serving as a proxy for a values debate. Marjorie Heins, director of the Free Expression Policy Project at the National Coalition Against Censorship and author of *Not in Front of the Children: "Indecency," Censorship, and the Innocence of Youth*, puts it this way: "If you're convinced that certain attitudes and values are wrong, then you consider exposing a child to those values a harm in itself."

The Second-Parent Trap

Even on the assumption that heterosexual households are somehow better for children, some restrictions on gay parenting are hard to fathom. For children in Florida's foster care system, the alternative to gay parents may be no parents at all. And many policies don't *prevent* gay couples from raising children; they just make life *more difficult* for gay parents and their children.

Barriers to second-parent adoption in some slates create a variety of difficulties for gay couples raising children, often allowing only one to be recognized as a legal parent. Allison Bauer is an attorney who sits on the board of the Family Pride Coalition, an advocacy group for gay families. She lived in Virginia before moving to Massachusetts, where she could adopt her partner Marie Longo's biological children, twin girls. During the pregnancy, says Bauer, "we told our friends that if Marie went into labor, they should drive her into D.C. and *then* call an ambulance—we knew D.C. would issue an amended birth certificate with both our names later, and Virginia wouldn't." Until they moved, she adds, "I spent 14 months holding my breath. One night when the kids were six months old, Rebecca woke up with a terrible barking cough. We knew it was croup, and I had to wake Marie up because I was afraid the hospital would question my authority to authorize care, even though I had a document that gave me power of attorney."

Such fears are why Anne Magro is fighting to overturn an Oklahoma law stipulating that "this state, any of its agencies, or any court of this state shall not recognize an adoption by more than one individual of the same sex from any other state or foreign jurisdiction." Magro, an accounting professor at the University of Oklahoma, had moved from New Jersey, where the state had granted her partner of 13 years, Heather Finstuen, second-parent rights over Magro's biological daughters.

Oklahoma state Rep. Thad Balkman (R-Norman), who supported the adoption law, defends it as a "reflection of our public policy that we support one-man-one-woman adoptions. To grant privileges like birth certificates to people who aren't in that relationship is doublespeak; we have to be consistent." Yet Balkman also claims that all the rights "so-called parents" have when their adoptions are recognized can be obtained through other means, such as by obtaining durable power of attorney for the second parent.

Brian Chase, an attorney with the gay rights litigation firm Lambda Legal who is representing Magro and Finstuen, disagrees. "A final adoption decree entitles a child to Social Security benefits and medical benefits that can't be conferred by a power of attorney," he says. "Furthermore, the most important right guaranteed by a final adoption is the right to continue to care for a child if something were to happen to the other parent. No power of attorney or will confers the degree of security that accompanies an adoption." And such workarounds, Magro adds, are often complex, time-consuming, and expensive.

New York University law professor Linda J. Silberman, an expert in interjudicial legal conflicts, believes policies like Oklahoma's may violate the Constitution's Full Faith and

Credit Clause, which says "Full Faith and Credit shall be given in each State to the public Acts, Records, and judicial Proceedings of every other State." "If you're talking about one state applying another state's *law*," Silberman explains, "there's a public policy exception. If you have a court judgment from another state, though, you can't just say 'oh, we have a different public policy' and ignore it on that basis."

But the 1996 Defense of Marriage Act stipulates that "the United States Constitution shall not be construed to require any state or territory to give effect to any public act, record, or judicial proceeding respecting a relationship between persons of the same sex that is treated as a marriage under the laws of another state or territory." That attempt to reach judicial proceedings, normally not subject to "public policy exceptions," adds a new wrinkle, says Silberman. A state hostile to gay rights might, for instance, refuse to recognize a custody ruling from another state that allowed civil unions. . . .

Family Values

On a drizzly weekend at the end of April [2005], some 250 gay parents, prospective parents, and their kids gathered at Sligo Middle School in Silver Spring, Maryland, for a daylong Family Pride Coalition conference on gay parenting. Standing under a scrolling rainbow LED marquee announcing "Congratulations, Honor Roll Students," Cayo Gamber, a writing professor at George Washington University, surveyed the day's dense program and quipped: "It would be wonderful if straight people came to parenting with this kind of scrutiny. . . . For us it's a choice, not an accident or a destiny."

At a breakout workshop on adoption, a few dozen participants studied the details of that choice. Panelists related their experiences adopting through private agencies, through foster care, and from the shrinking number of foreign countries open to gay parents. They recounted spending tens of thousands of dollars, waiting anxious months, sitting through lengthy and intrusive interviews and "home studies," and filling out mountains of paperwork in a process one likened to "buying a house and applying to grad school simultaneously."

Ask a child in foster care which makes him feel more threatened: the thought of being raised by homosexuals, or the prospect of an indefinite number of years spent passing through an indefinite number of homes.

The hearts of conservatives would, one might think, be warmed by such a group. They feel the universal human need for family as deeply and acutely as anyone and are unusually determined to make committed parenting a central part of their lives.

Those behind the burgeoning assault on gay parenting would have us believe these people are a menace to the children they would take in. And had any of them visited Sligo Middle School that afternoon, they surely would have heard their share of complaints from the children and teenagers in attendance: complaints about homophobic teachers, about classmates whose peers and parents have taught them to use *gay* as an epithet. Concerned conservatives might ask those kids: Are those complaints a sign there's something wrong with your gay families, or with the broader culture?

Better still, they could visit Florida and ask a child in foster care which makes him feel more threatened: the thought of being raised by homosexuals, or the prospect of an indefinite number of years spent passing through an indefinite number of homes. They could ask whether "family values" are best served by attempting to marginalize gay couples who raise families, by "protecting" abused or sick children from people who want to give them a home, by forcing parents to worry whether they'll have the legal authority to bring their kids to the hospital in an emergency. They could ask Charlie.

5

Gay Adoption Is Not in the Best Interest of Children

Ed Vitagliano

Ed Vitagliano is the director of research for American Family Association, a Mississippi-based nonprofit organization that represents traditional family values and focuses on the influences of mass media. He is also news editor of AFA Journal, *the association's monthly publication.*

As the battle over gay adoption intensifies, homosexual activists argue that science is on their side. However, these scientific studies do not meet acceptable standards of psychological research, while others conclude that children raised by gay and lesbian parents are more likely to identify as gay. Moreover, heterosexual parenting is in the best interest for children because mothers and fathers have distinctive qualities innate to gender that are necessary for child development. Along with couples nearing divorce or who are unemployed, gay adoption is a less than optimal arrangement, tragedies and heart-wrenching rhetoric aside.

In what some are calling a "second front" in the culture war—trailing in the wake of same-sex marriage—the battle over gay adoption is increasing in intensity.

Currently Florida is the only state that officially bans gay adoption, a law that has been upheld in federal court despite an intense publicity campaign, orchestrated by lesbian actress Rosie O'Donnell, to have it overturned.

Ed Vitagliano, "A Difference Worth Embracing: Why Mother-Father Couples Are Superior to Gay Couples When It Comes to Adoption," *American Family Association Journal,* June 2006. Reproduced by permission.

However, in 16 states efforts are underway to put gay adoption bans on the November [2006] ballot. And both sides are trying to convince the public to see things their way.

Gay Parents Under the Microscope

The core argument put forth by homosexual activists is that science is on their side. They claim that scientific studies demonstrate that kids raised by gay couples suffer no adverse consequences from the experience, and that there is therefore no risk in allowing homosexuals to adopt.

But the research says no such thing, according to Dr. Timothy J. Dailey, senior fellow in culture studies at the Family Research Council. Much of it "fails to meet acceptable standards for psychological research; it is compromised by methodological flaws and driven by political agendas instead of an objective search for truth," he insists.

For example, Drs. Robert Lerner and Althea Nagai, partners in a social science research consulting firm, examined 49 of the studies most commonly used to defend same-sex parenting and adoption. In their report, *No basis: What the studies don't tell us about same-sex parenting*, the pair "found at least one fatal flaw in all 49 studies," indicating that "no generalizations can reliably be made based on any of these studies. For these reasons the studies are no basis for good science or good public policy."

Moreover, there is evidence that kids raised in same-sex households are more likely to drift towards the sexual orientation of their gay parents.

Dr. Judith Stacey, a sociologist at the University of Southern California and a supporter of gay adoption, admitted in a 2002 *Primetime Thursday* (ABC) interview that research had shown that children raised by homosexual couples were more likely to have "either considered or had one same-sex experience" than children raised by heterosexuals.

The study to which Stacey referred (Fiona Tasker, Susan Golombok, "Adults Raised as Children in Lesbian Families," *American Journal of Orthopsychiatry*, 4/95) actually found that 24% of children raised by lesbian mothers had "been involved in a same-gender sexual relationship," while none of the kids who had been raised by heterosexuals reported such same-sex activity.

Children raised by gay parents are also more likely to perceive themselves as gay. In a 1994 article in *American Sociological Review*, Stacey said the Tasker-Golombok results showed "the young adults reared by lesbian mothers were also significantly more likely to report having thought they might experience homoerotic attraction or relationships." The differences were "striking," she added, because 64% of the young adults raised by same-sex parents said they had considered having a same-sex relationship, as opposed to 17% of those raised by heterosexuals.

The Tasker-Golombok study also revealed that the percentage of the young women raised by lesbians who later went on to self-identify as lesbians was nearly *eight times* the rate of the general population (11% versus 1.4%).

As Stacey wrote in her *American Sociological Review* piece, "The evidence, while scanty and underanalyzed, hints that parental sexual orientation is positively associated with the possibility that children will be more likely to attain a similar orientation—and theory and common sense also support such a view."

The Male-Female Model

Ironically, it is usually traditionalists who point to "common sense" when it comes to the subject of gay adoption. They have argued that it makes sense to believe that a child will do *best* in a home with their biological mother *and* father.

Why? Dailey says there is a "well-established and growing body of evidence showing that both mothers and fathers provide unique and irreplaceable contributions to the raising of children." That is, mothers and fathers parent differently.

Glenn T. Stanton, senior research analyst for marriage and family at Focus on the Family and author of *Why Marriage Matters: Reasons to Believe in Marriage in Postmodern Society*, agrees. He says research demonstrates that there are a host of differences in the way in which mothers and fathers interact with their children, from the manner in which they play with kids, to the way they communicate, to the way they prepare children for life.

For example, Stanton says that by eight weeks of age, even infants can tell the difference between a male and a female interacting with them because fathers "have a distinct style of communication and interaction with children."

The differences between maternal and paternal parenting may well be biological and not simply a product of socialization, according to research results released by the Society for Neuroscience (SfN).

"Conventional wisdom has long suggested that mothers are more attuned to infants, especially their own, than are fathers," said Dr. Jeffrey Lorberbaum, who conducted one SfN study, with colleagues at the Medical University of South Carolina. "Our studies suggest that this may be true."

Thus, as common sense would suggest—and research is demonstrating—fathers don't mother, and mothers don't father.

Take parental discipline, Stanton says. Research shows that "fathers stress justice, fairness and duty (based on rules), while mothers stress sympathy, care and help (based on relationships). Fathers tend to observe and enforce rules systematically and sternly, which teaches children the objectivity and consequences of right and wrong. Mothers tend toward grace and sympathy in the midst of disobedience, which provides a sense of hopefulness. Again, either of these by themselves is not good, but together, they create a healthy, proper balance."

As a result of these innate differences, then, what a mother and father both bring to the home are important and necessary. Dailey insists that the research reveals that "[c]hildren raised in traditional families by a mother and father are happier, healthier and more successful than children raised in non-traditional environments."

If true, this would mean that a pairing of same-sex adults cannot replace the male-female model. "They say that the only thing that children need is two loving adults to care for them, but no matter how loving two dads may be they simply can't provide a mommy to a child," says Focus on the Family psychologist Dr. Bill Maier.

Nobody Available to Adopt?

However, the trump card tossed onto the table by homosexual activists is an emotionally laden one: children without homes, languishing in the foster care system. Regardless of what may be best for kids in terms of parental models or parental ideals, they argue, the current situation is so bad that our society can't afford to be picky.

As Dahlia Lithwick, senior editor and legal correspondent for *Slate*, says, those who want to ban gay adoption "must thus argue . . . that it's better for these children to languish in state custody, or bounce from foster home to foster home, than be raised by gay parents who want them."

Admittedly, this is a card that is hard to beat because too often in our culture, emotion does trump sound policy.

However, according to Robert Knight, director of the Culture and Family Institute, an affiliate of Concerned Women for America, the issue is not a clear-cut winner for the homosexual lobby—at least not when one considers the actual numbers involved.

Knight says there are about 600,000 children in the U.S. foster care system at any given time, but at least half of these are caught up in custody battles and would not be candidates for adoption anyway.

On the other hand, Knight says that the National Council on Adoption puts the number of mother-father, married couples waiting to adopt at between one and two million. These married couples "are having such difficulty [adopting] in the U.S. that they are seeking children, at great expense, in Russia, China, Romania and other nations," he said. "There is no excuse for deliberately placing a child in a motherless or fatherless household by design, except under unusual circumstances."

Banning gay adoptions is not the same as saying that every gay couple would be worse than every straight couple, but that most of the time the best place to put kids is with a mother and father.

True, of the 300,000 kids who are available for adoption, some would be unadoptable, being too old, perhaps, or having special needs that would scare away most couples wanting to adopt.

In the end, however, sad situations and heart-wrenching circumstances cannot determine public policy, which, after all, must be based on sound principles, and not exceptions. For example, even with unadoptable kids still in the foster care system, we would not want to place those children with a couple on the verge of divorce, or with two unemployed adults. This is not because such adults are unloving or incapable of being good parents, but because public policies must consider what is optimal—and less than optimal—*most* of the time.

Likewise, banning gay adoptions is not the same as saying that every gay couple would be worse than every straight couple, but that most of the time the *best* place to put kids is with a mother and father.

The difference between mother and father, therefore, is a difference worth embracing as a society. Kids deserve the best, and a mom and a dad best fit the bill.

6

Parents Should Accept Their Gay and Lesbian Children's Sexual Orientation

John Pugh

John Pugh lives in Perth, Australia. He and his wife, Margaret, initiated the first Parents and Friends of Lesbians and Gays in Western Australia in 1989. The Pughs have two sons, one of whom is gay.

When a son or daughter comes out to the family, there will be tears, secrecy, frustration, confusion, and disapproval from the community or church. Parents, however, should accept their child's sexuality. This can be a long process of reflection and self-education, but they will learn that homosexuality is normal, that how they raised their son or daughter has no effect on this issue, and that the gay community—especially other parents—can offer support and joy. Parents should also be supportive of their gay or lesbian child's relationships and be thankful that he or she has found love. Those who reject their child's sexuality do it out of selfishness—accepting a gay or lesbian child is a true test of a parent's love.

On a warm autumn day in March 1980, something was about to happen that would change the whole course of our family's life, something we never dreamed could possibly happen to us.

John Pugh, "Letters," *My Child Is Gay: How Parents React When They Hear the News*, edited by Bryce MacDougall, St. Leonards, NSW, Australia: Allen & Unwin, 2006, pp. 3–10. Copyright © 1998, 2006 by Bryce McDougall. All rights reserved. Reproduced by permission of Allen & Unwin, www.allenandunwin.com.

Jeff, our son, had been a bit 'uptight' for some time, but when he went off one day and didn't come home all night, by next morning my wife, Margaret, and I were naturally a bit worried. By lunchtime we were really concerned, but on hearing his car come into the driveway, a great feeling of relief came over us.

After some time, we were puzzled that he had not come inside and I was about to go out and voice my concern on his overnight absence. Margaret, however, restrained me, in a mother's knowing way, and said that we should wait a little while longer.

'I've got something to tell you,' Jeff said, when he finally came inside, 'perhaps you had better sit down.'

We seated ourselves in our lounge, Margaret next to Jeff and myself nearby. Many thoughts raced through my mind in those next few moments: drugs, trouble with a girl (on reflection, this thought is now quite funny), a felony of some kind, money problems—what could be worrying him? It was obvious something had him deeply troubled.

Then, with that tiny phrase 'I'm gay', our world was turned upside down.

A New Course

From that moment our lives started on a new course, which was to bring untold tears, secrecy, frustration, confusion and also intense annoyance with people and their attitudes. We would, however, eventually find many new friends and a great joy that we have only found in the gay community.

In the minutes that followed Jeff's disclosure, we asked all the questions that parents seem to ask, I guess.

'How do you know you're gay?'

'How long have you known?'

'Are you sure? Perhaps you may change your mind later on.'

'Have you told anyone else?'

'No.'

I remember saying, 'Isn't it wrong?'—something that I felt deeply sorry about afterwards. He gave us answers that we didn't particularly want to hear.

On that first day I guess we blundered around, somewhat stunned and not knowing what to do. Who could we talk to about homosexuality? Maybe we could find someone who would tell us it may only be a passing phase. Foolishly, I thought Jeff might change his mind when he found out what it was really all about.

In my ignorance I imagined that a "good woman" was the answer for a gay man and likewise a "good man" the answer for a lesbian woman.

Our elder son, Graeme, was out visiting his fiancée, Sue, at the time, so we rang him and asked him to come home because a family crisis had developed that we couldn't discuss over the phone. After arriving home and expressing his disbelief at the news, he suggested that we try to contact Gayline. So he and Margaret went across the road, to a public phone box, to be out of earshot, and rang Gayline.

The man on the phone only confirmed our worst fears. He said, 'If Jeff is 21 and has done a lot of soul-searching [as he said he had] and has come to the conclusion that he is gay, then to imagine him being able to live his life as heterosexual is quite impossible.' He said that we had to change our lives to accommodate the new person that had come into our midst.

Looking back, two things that the man on Gayline said proved to be very important to us at the time.

1. 'It is OK to be gay, you know.'

2. 'You, as parents, must be very special for Jeff to have come out to you first. Most gay people are afraid to do this because they fear their parents will react badly. Initially, they usually tell only siblings and close friends.'

I guess, at the time, this gave us a little lift. Many gay people that we have met over the years since have told us this. What they fear most about coming out is the adverse reaction of family members, particularly parents. Jeff said, years later, in a radio interview, that coming out to Mum and Dad was the hardest thing he had ever done.

At first we had many sleepless nights, wondering what to do. We realised that we knew so very little about homosexuality. We had never had the strong antagonism that lots of folk seem to have towards these 'other people', but, like many, we gave it little thought because it didn't concern us. In my ignorance I imagined that a 'good woman' was the answer for a gay man and likewise a 'good man' the answer for a lesbian woman. I certainly had a very long way to go.

A Long Self-Educating Process

So we began searching for information about homosexuality and commenced a long self-educating process. This gave us a much deeper understanding of homosexual people and their problems and changed many ideas and beliefs that we previously held, especially about sexuality in general. However, finding any positive reading matter in 1980 proved to be very difficult. Very little gay literature was readily available at that time. Besides, it's very hard to ask in libraries and bookshops for books about something that you are afraid to talk about. Nevertheless, in time we did become more bold, the fears gradually left us and our library of gay books grew steadily.

In the meantime, Graeme, in fear and concern, had to explain things to Sue. She was a close friend of Jeff, too, and although completely surprised, she took it in her stride. Jeff was her friend and whether he was straight or gay made no difference to her. She went to the top in our estimation. Jeff was best man at Graeme and Sue's wedding and there has been a strong bond between them ever since. This bond was extended to Jeff's partner, Graham, when he joined the family.

Now there are children, and uncles Jeff and Graham are a popular part of their lives too. I anticipate and hope that they will grow up free of any prejudice towards homosexual people.

Until this time, we thought of ourselves as a happy, fairly normal, middle-class, suburban family—maybe we were a bit smug and complacent. Margaret and I both worked full-time. We were both very involved with and held positions in the Uniting Church. Our social life revolved around the church. However, our boys had long since decided that the church had no interest for them and we accepted that.

There are still tears, frustration, and sometimes intense annoyance at the attitudes of some people, particularly "Christians," show toward the homosexual issue and the gay people we have grown to love.

Our own disillusionment with the church probably began when AIDS raised its ugly head. The church had to be seen as caring for people with AIDS, but it was very careful not to be seen as accepting homosexuality. We tried, for some time, to educate people by becoming involved in various groups. Some people understood, but mostly they just felt sorry that we had this 'dreadful problem', a gay son. As time went by we became interested and involved with the Universal Fellowship of Metropolitan Community Churches. The MCC was founded, in 1969, in the USA by the Reverend Troy Perry, who was rejected by his own church because he was gay. It is now a rapidly growing church, particularly in America but also throughout the world. In the MCC we found a love and acceptance that we had not felt before in any other church to which we had belonged.

For a time, Margaret and I were involved in the Social Justice Working Group of the Uniting Church, and amongst the group members we found some wonderful support. However, one of the members told us once that the Social Justice group was the most hated group of the Uniting Church and naturally we came to this conclusion ourselves too. I guess, in the end we realised that all that was to be gained from the church was sympathy, not acceptance and understanding. Sympathy alone was something we could do without. So after much painful deliberation, we eventually severed our connection with the Uniting Church and started to direct our energy towards places where we felt the real need existed, like PFLAG [Parents and Friends of Lesbians and Gays] and MCC.

We still feel that although the churches may be talking about the acceptance of homosexuality, when it comes to voting to accept openly homosexual persons, they will eventually back away. We hope we are proved wrong.

When [former Australian Pastor] Michael Chamberlain was asked in an interview if he had lost his faith, he said, 'No! but I have lost the baggage that went with it.' After shedding some of our baggage, we now feel privileged that we have been allowed to share in the love, joy, friendship, sufferings and sadness of the gay community. Unfortunately, however, there are still tears, frustration and sometimes intense annoyance at the attitudes some people, particularly 'Christians', show towards the homosexual issue and the gay people we have grown to love.

For a year or two after Jeff came out, I searched deeply, trying to find a reason for him becoming gay. Was there something we, as parents, had done or hadn't done? Had we treated him badly or differently from his elder brother? Had there been some major crisis that could have caused a psychological upset? Jeff assured us that the answer to all these questions was, 'No!' Nothing we had done or should have done would have made any difference.

As I saw it, Jeff had a good and perfectly normal childhood. He gave his mother few problems being born. Somehow we knew it was going to be a boy—even the doctor said so—despite the lack of ultrasound in those days. I guess most parents do their learning on the firstborn, so he had the benefit of some experience on our part. Although different in nature from his brother, he was still very much a boy. He developed the usual boisterous nature that boys have, managing to get hurt on many occasions. He loved his teddy bear and soon developed an attraction for toy cars and things mechanical. Of course, toys needed to be tough to survive rough treatment but we thought he was overdoing things when he tested the strength of a Matchbox toy in a workshop vice.

Jeff was always generous by nature and his money box always had to be accessible. If it wasn't, it was soon made to be, so he was usually broke. However, none of our family ever went without a birthday or Christmas present, even if it meant borrowing money to buy one. His membership in Cub and Scouts led to him becoming a Pack Leader, but his interest in Scouting waned a few years after joining a senior Scouts group.

Jeff was never keen on sporting activity but probably compensated, to some extent, by doing very well academically, winning top-of-the-class awards in two subjects in his final year at high school and gaining his Bachelor of Business degree with distinction.

Like most siblings, Jeff and Graeme fought with each other most of their young lives, but almost overnight, when they were fourteen and sixteen years old, their fighting stopped. We've often wondered why. Since then they've been good friends. From primary school days, both boys had positive ideas on their careers. Accounting was Jeff's aim in life and motor mechanics that of his brother. Both achieved their ambitions and have continued in these careers.

In the early times, we knew very little about gay relationships, and were a little concerned at what Jeff might do to this end. However, he had his own ideas on finding a partner, and this was by advertising in one of the local newspapers. So, in this way, he met Graham.

After Graeme and Sue were married, Jeff stayed on living at home for a month or so and one day casually asked us if we would mind if he moved out into a flat of his own. Naturally, we said that would be OK, as long as he was happy doing that. 'Oh well,' he said, 'as long as you don't mind, I'll be going now.' Anticipating our reply, he had things packed and was ready to leave.

So, all of a sudden, our family was gone, leaving Margaret and me with the strange, empty feeling you get when they all finally leave. You're glad, in a way, to see them go but deeply sad that they are not there to care for any more. All the activities that a family generates suddenly stop and a strange quiet seems to descend. Now both boys had gone, our elder son Graeme with his new wife and Jeff to a new friend unknown to us.

We first met Graham some time later when Jeff persuaded him to come to dinner with us one evening. He said he came trembling with fear. Naturally, we were concerned that Jeff may have teamed up with someone we would dislike. However, we should have had enough trust in Jeff's judgment to know he wouldn't choose just anyone. We took an immediate liking to Graham and he grew steadily to be like one of our family.

I believe the love we profess to have for our children is truly tested when we first hear that little phrase, "I'm gay," from one of them.

Apart from Graham's mum, it would be a few years before we met two other parents. With them and a number of gay people and their families we formed a small support group, Uniting Friends. But where were all the other parents? Our small group eventually disbanded, but during the fight for homosexual law reform in Western Australia in 1989–90, we joined in the parliamentary debate with many gays and lesbians and some parents. From this campaign, together with our friend June, we gathered together the parents of lesbians and gays that we knew and on 2 December 1989 PFLAG was born in Western Australia. A year or two later, one of the group members, Heather, moved to Sydney and started a PFLAG group there. PFLAG is now spreading throughout Australia.

So our dream for many years at last became a reality. A support group for parents at our own time of need would have been so wonderful.

Purely Selfish Matters

I still get angry at parents who cannot or will not accept their child's homosexuality. Maybe they can't understand, but many won't even try. I still don't fully understand, all these years later. I guess that I never will, because I'm heterosexual. However, there is no real reason for parents to refuse to accept a gay son or lesbian daughter. What many people give as excuses are purely selfish matters that will upset their own lives and relationships. Isn't the life of a son or daughter worth more than that? I believe that the love we profess to have for our children is truly tested when we first hear that little phrase, 'I'm gay', from one of them. How we behave then will reflect the true depth of that love we profess to have.

Margaret and I are so grateful that Jeff had the courage to tell us first about his homosexuality. In retrospect, however, we were so sorry that he carried the burden alone for all of his teenage years.

We are happy that he has found a soul mate in Graham and that they have worked hard at maintaining a lasting, loving relationship.

I like to think that Jeff knew we loved him a lot when he first came out, and that he knew we would accept him, as he was, no matter what. I like to think that he was right.

7

Parents of a Homosexual Child Should Uphold Own View of Homosexuality

Joe Dallas

Joe Dallas is former president of Exodus International, a nonprofit Christian organization that promotes freedom from homosexuality through Christian values, teachings, and beliefs. He is also author of Desires in Conflict, A Strong Delusion, *and* When Homosexuality Hits Home: What to Do When a Loved One Says They're Gay, *from which the following viewpoint is excerpted.*

Parents with a homosexual son or daughter should not compromise their Christian views and are advised to take steps in approaching this issue. First, parents should determine their child's position on homosexuality. Second, parents should clarify that their own views are unchangeable but assure their son or daughter of their support. Third, parents should ask questions about their child's lifestyle and express their fears, such as the high rates of HIV and at-risk behavior among homosexuals, while refraining from assumptions. These steps will enhance communication and trust between the parents and child and help set the expectations and boundaries to come in the future.

You, for example, are probably looking at your relationship with your son or daughter under a microscope. You're examining the early years, perhaps in light of theories you've

Joe Dallas, "Chapter 3: Loving a Gay Son or Daughter," *When Homosexuality Hits Home: What to Do When a Loved One Says They're Gay,* Eugene, OR: Harvest House Publishers, 2004, pp. 73–74, 80–86. Copyright © 2004 Joe Dallas. All rights reserved. Used by permission of Harvest House Publishers, Eugene, OR, www.harvesthousepublishers.com.

read on homosexuality, and you're wondering: Did she get enough love? Were my spouse and I affectionate enough with her? Did she get enough time, attention, discipline, prayer, concern? Did I tell her often enough how much I loved her? Was I all, as a parent, I could have been?

And the answer, of course, is no. No child was raised as well as he could have been. The question, then, isn't whether or not you failed in any way. You did, as we all have and will. The question is whether or not your imperfections caused your son or daughter to become homosexual.

And again, the answer is no, because homosexuality is not caused by one influence alone. . . . [T]here's a constellation of influences involved. Based on all available research, when we try to pinpoint what creates homosexuality, we find at least five factors:

1. The child's genes (whether or not he's born with a genetic susceptibility to gender-identity problems) combined with:

2. His relationship with his parents combined with:

3. His relationship with siblings and peers combined with:

4. Possible violations or traumas combined with:

5. Other factors we're still unaware of

Perhaps some or all of these combined, not one of these alone, create the homosexual orientation.

Now let's take a worst-case view of your parenting. Suppose your relationship with your son or daughter fit the developmental theory mentioned in the previous chapter. Suppose that, as a father, you were emotionally distant from your son; or as a mother, you were too dominant or over involved in his life. Or, if your daughter is lesbian, you as a mother were uninvolved; or as her father, you were overinvolved or somehow abusive. In that case, you may be part of the problem—(notice factor 2 above)—but only *part*. Other factors beyond your control, such as factors 1, 3, 4, and 5, also may have come into play. So the worst you could say in such a case is that your relationship was faulty and may have *contributed to*, but not *created*, your son's or daughter's homosexuality. (Remember, after all, many heterosexuals were raised by parents who fit the above patterns.)

Likewise, let's take a best-case viewpoint. Suppose, imperfect as you may be, your parenting was exemplary by any reasonable standard. You loved your child, and the balance of affection and discipline in your home was right about where it should have been. That alone can't prevent factors 1, 3, 4, and 5 from happening, can it? So your parenting may, in fact, have very little to do with the situation. . . .

When someone says, "I'm gay," that doesn't answer the question as to how the person feels about homosexuality, and why.

Meanwhile, you and your child still have a relationship to preserve. So, to help you and your loved one set terms for the future of your relationship, let me offer some suggestions for *clarifying* three points.

1. Clarify Your Son's or Daughter's *Position* on Homosexuality

Ascertain where he or she stands on homosexuality by asking: Have you decided this is normal and moral, or are you still deciding? And on what basis will you make, or have you made, this decision?

When someone says, "I'm gay," that doesn't answer the question as to how the person feels about homosexuality, and why. In other words, two questions are primary: Has the person truly decided he's attracted to the same sex, and is he what we'll call gay-affirming? *Gay-affirming* means "holding a belief that homosexuality is normal and legitimate." So "I'm gay" can mean any of the following:

Decided and gay-affirming: "I'm gay, that's fine with me, and I'm waiting for Mom and Dad to finally accept it."

Undecided: "I'm attracted to the same sex, but I'm not sure whether or not it's okay to act on these attractions. I'm still deciding, but I at least want to be honest about the existence of these attractions."

Decided but not gay-affirming: "These attractions are definitely here, but I know homosexuality is wrong, so I don't intend to act on them. I intend to resist them."

To get a better understanding of where your relationship with your son or daughter is headed, ask which of the above best describes him or her.

If he is decided but not gay-affirming:

That means he is, in essence, admitting that homosexuality is a *temptation*, but he's also rejecting it as a *way of life*. Offer your wholehearted support and appreciation for his honesty. Make sure he knows you're aware of how hard it is to say no to something the rest of the world seems to be saying is normal, and reassure him he has an ally and friend in you. . . .

If she is undecided:

Ask candidly on what basis she will be making her decision. Scripture? Her feelings? Professional or academic opinion? Don't ask with the goal of challenging her answer—make it clear you only want to better understand how she will come to one of the most momentous decisions she'll ever make.

Ask if she's open to talking to a Christian counselor or pastor whose viewpoint may be more traditional and who can offer a different perspective than the one she's probably been hearing. . . .

But if she prefers not to, I strongly suggest you not push it. I've seen too many parents pressure their grown sons or daughters into counseling, with predictably bad results. I can virtually guarantee you that, if you push her or him into a counselor's office, you will not only *not* get the desired results, but your son or daughter will resent you deeply for the intrusion.

If he is decided and gay-affirming:

Ask what, if anything, he's expecting of you. Agreement? Discussion? Conversion to his way of thinking? Again, the goal here is not to start an argument but rather to get a better idea of his expectations. This will help you clarify your own position and negotiate the relationship from here on.

Don't beat a dead horse by repeating, every time you see your son or daughter, what the Bible says and why you disapprove of homosexuality.

---

2. Clarify Your Own Position on Homosexuality

Don't beat a dead horse by repeating, every time you see your son or daughter, what the Bible says and why you disapprove of homosexuality. That's unnecessary. But make certain you've clarified, once and for all, where you stand. . . . Let me also suggest you make sure your son or daughter knows the following:

- You know he or she didn't ask for these feelings.

- You appreciate his or her honesty.

- Your position on the matter is still unchangeable.

- You want to protect your relationship through mutual respect and, as much as possible, mutual understanding.

- You may never agree on this issue, but you're committed to not letting that disagreement ruin your relationship.

3. Clarify Your Fears

"I'm scared to death now that my son has told me he's gay," I've often heard. "I'm worried about AIDS, but I also fear for his future. I've read about high rates of alcoholism and abuse among gays and lesbians and that their relationships don't tend to last. So now that he's come out, what should I expect his life to be like?"

While there are several things to fear, there's no reason to believe all the things you fear for your son or daughter will inevitably happen.

True, the rate of HIV infection remains much higher among homosexual men in America than among heterosexuals. But not every man who is homosexual is sexually active; not every homosexual who is sexually active engages in the sexual practices that transmit the AIDS virus. So it would be a grave mistake to assume your son is in immediate danger just because of his recent disclosure. What brings risk into his life is not his homosexual orientation, but how he chooses to conduct himself sexually.

Likewise, no matter what you've heard about the gay lifestyle, remember, there is a good deal of variety in the lifestyles of homosexual men and women. Many gays are very promiscuous; many aren't. Some settle into long-term relationships; some have short-lived affairs; still others prefer lifelong celibacy.

For that matter, there really is no such thing as a typical homosexual person. While most seem to be politically liberal, many are, in fact, conservative. Some are flamboyant and easily recognized; many are entirely unrecognizable. So at this point, please do *not* assume your daughter or son is going to live a certain way just because you've heard of the way some, or even many, homosexuals live.

Instead of assuming, *ask*. Ask how he or she lives. Tell your loved one plainly what your fears are and ask if he or she can help you by answering your questions honestly. That will give you a more accurate portrait of what you can expect, which can only help to ease family tensions and misunderstanding. I've known cases in which this approach has been more than helpful.

One mother, for example, came to me for a consultation. She was living with a twofold dread. First, she dreaded the problems she thought her son would have as a young gay man, problems she had both read and heard about. After he came out to her, she had picked up several books on male homosexuality, most of them written from a Christian perspective. While there was much valuable information in these books, they had also frightened her by offering statistics on the prevalence of promiscuity among gay men and the chances that disease, alcoholism, suicide, violence, and drug use could plague her son as well. No wonder she lived in fear! Thoughts of her son's engaging in dangerous, bizarre activities became a source of daily torment.

But she was just as tormented by the fear of losing him. They'd already argued about homosexuality, and their positions were clear: He was gay, she disapproved; but she had agreed not to badger him. Afterward she started hearing the stories and reading the materials about gay men, which terrified her. But since she'd promised to drop the subject, she stifled the urge to talk to him about his lifestyle and, more specifically, her concerns. She was trapped between her promise to respect his choices and her need to better understand what those choices were.

I suggested it was possible to ask these questions without "preaching." She wasn't, after all, trying to change him, as much as she was trying to understand. So in an honest and tearful conversation, she told him:

> "I know you've decided you're gay, and I'm not trying to change you. But I've read that so many gay men have hundreds of partners, and that they're in danger of AIDS and other diseases, as well as drug use. Can you at least tell me if

that's true? Do you use drugs? Do you have several partners? Honey, please just help me understand how you live, because I'm so worried!"

Far from being offended, her son was moved by her concerns and was happy to relieve them. He was not promiscuous, never used drugs, drank occasionally, and knew all the do's and don'ts about unprotected sex.

This wasn't entirely satisfying to her. She wasn't convinced there was such a thing as safe sex, and she brought up realistic concerns about condom effectiveness and breakage. And knowing that her son lived a responsible life in many ways couldn't negate her objections to his homosexuality. Still, it was a huge relief to learn he did not fit the profile of a reckless, hedonistic young man flirting with death.

God holds out hope, *for both you and your children.*

So clarify your fears. Doing so can only enhance communication and trust between you and your child.

These three clarifications, then, will help you know what to expect of your son or daughter at this point. They also will give you an idea of what sorts of things you'll need to negotiate. . . .

But before moving on, as the parent of a prodigal, will you take a moment to review Jeremiah's words—God's words, really—to parents in pain?

> Refrain thy voice from weeping, and thine eyes from tears: for thy work shall be rewarded, saith the LORD; and they [your children] shall come again from the land of the enemy. And there is hope in thine end, saith the LORD, that thy children shall come again to their own border. (Jeremiah 31:16–17)

You can't miss the threefold message here:

God *sees.* He sees both your beloved daughter or son, and He sees your tears.

God *perseveres*. He continues His efforts long after human effort has exhausted itself.

God holds out *hope*, for both you and your children.

So in confidence of His ongoing work in your adult gay loved ones, you can now begin negotiating the boundaries of your relationship.

8

Gay Marriage in California Establishes Equal Rights

Los Angeles Times Opinion Column

Founded in 1881, the Los Angeles Times *is a Pulitzer Prize–winning daily California newspaper.*

The decision of the California Supreme Court to recognize gay marriage upholds, not diminishes, its bonds. Because of this victory for equal rights, gay and lesbian couples in California are finally given the public protections and vows needed to sustain long-term relationships. Opponents argue that gay marriage threatens traditional unions and the institution of marriage. On the contrary, as it was with interracial marriage, the legalization of gay marriage is not a question of right or wrong, but of whether those who condemn it have the right to deny it to others. In essence, gay marriage celebrates love and establishes equality, and in doing so does not diminish the vows and beauty of heterosexual marriage.

Across California today [June 17, 2008], in mass public weddings and in small, private services, gay and lesbian couples will exchange official vows of undying love and wedlock. With the sanction of the state Supreme Court, these couples stand together as full citizens at last.

Their long odyssey to reach this day serves to remind us why people marry at all, especially in an era of casual relationships. As any married person can attest, marriage is significant precisely because it is difficult. True, it confers certain public protections, but even more, it requires personal sacrifices. If mutual affection and appreciation were enough to sustain relationships across the years, there would be no need for solemn vows of fidelity. Those vows protect many a marriage through many a rough patch; when two people agree to enter into such a union, it by rights should carry the name and honor of marriage, whether it's between people of opposite sex or between a man and a man, or a woman and a woman.

Opponents of same-sex marriage often deplore this expansion of the meaning of marriage because they view it as threatening to traditional unions. As they use this day as a rallying point for a proposed amendment to the state Constitution to ban such marriages, it's time to ask them directly: How does marriage of one type threaten others? Why do many heterosexuals feel that the beauty of their own marriage vows is in no way changed by today's weddings, while others feel theirs have somehow been diminished?

Perhaps the next few months will ease these fears, as same-sex couples begin their married lives together. Those couples will settle into communities without disorder or threat; they will bring legal protection to their bonds of love. Those bonds can only be good for society—children gain from being raised by married parents, and communities are stronger when residents are legally committed to one another. As more and more Californians marry, society will grow stronger, not weaker.

That's no doubt why opponents sought a stay of the court's ruling until after the election. They know that as same-sex marriages become commonplace, the fears about them will fade, and eventually we will wonder what all the fuss was about. In the meantime, opponents will resort to hyperbole and fear. Take this missive . . . from the Alliance for Marriage, issued in response to the announcement that the state of New York would recognize the unions performed in California:

> The governor of New York state will declare hundreds of years of marriage law in New York to be null and void. . . . The governor of New York state will force California-style 'gay marriage' on all the families and children of his own state.

It's a fairly reliable indicator of a bad argument when its proponent is forced to overstate the case in order to make it. The above surely qualifies. Same-sex couples are not upending the institution of marriage: nor are their supporters. Rather, they are engaged in a profoundly conservative act: They ask not to abolish marriage but to uphold it.

Some religious organizations won't perform these marriages or recognize these unions—that's their constitutional right. But the government, which has obligations of equity, may not engage in the discrimination that religions are allowed. As long as it bestows the privileges of marriage on some couples, it must bestow them on all.

For Those Who Disapprove

In California, the initiative process allows voters to amend the state Constitution directly, and unfortunately, a measure on the November [2008] ballot will give them the chance. The question won't be whether same-sex marriage is right or wrong—that's a matter of personal conviction—but whether those who believe it is wrong should have the power to deny marriage to those who seek its protections.

Put another way: Many Californians undoubtedly object to unwed couples who have and raise children together, but no constitutional amendment prevents that, whatever the moral calculus.

To those who insist that an unevolving morality undergirds our state and federal constitutions, we remind them that not so long ago, many Americans believed with passionate conviction that it was a sin, a threat to families and a violation of the law for people of different races to marry.

The 1969 ruling of a Virginia state court judge to deny this right to a black woman and a white man aptly summarized the fervor with which opponents of miscegenation drew on tradition and religion to support their views:

"Almighty God created the races white, black, yellow, malay and red, and he placed them on separate continents," trial judge Leon Bazile wrote. "And but for the interference with his arrangement there would be no cause for such marriages. The fact that he separated the races shows that he did not intend for the races to mix."

The U.S. Supreme Court struck down that ruling in 1967: On that happy day, 16 states were forced to abandon their laws banning interracial marriage. Today, interracial couples go about their lives without legal threat; some no doubt still feel the sting of disapproval. But those who would look askance on those lawfully wedded couples do so without the state to reinforce their bigotry. Our courts, certainly our supreme courts, exist not to assess God's will but to enforce the precepts of our constitutions, including the insistence that all Americans—black or white, male or female, straight or gay— are entitled to equal protection and the due process of our laws.

The California Supreme Court affirmed that principle [in May 2008] and delivered the eloquent basis for today's ceremonies. As the state's voters watch the celebrations in the coming months, they should enjoy the sight of fellow citizens availing themselves of a public institution, that of marriage. Those celebrations allow us to share in the newlyweds' happiness, to join in acknowledging a milestone of joy and lifelong commitment. And they prompt at least one more question for those who disapprove: How can the state's blessing on these acts of love in any way diminish us?

Gay Marriage in California Harms Society

David R. Usher

David R. Usher is a co-founder, legislative analyst, and President of the American Coalition for Fathers and Children, Missouri Coalition, an organization that promotes equal rights for all family members affected by divorce.

After California's Proposition 8 was passed, gays and lesbians showed "their true colors displaying great hate of heterosexuals." Some of this hatred, according to the author, comes from the the radical feminist movement, which sees marriage as "slavery for women" and lesbianism as a sign of true feminism. Usher claims that gay men are the political dupes of the radical feminists in their bid for the legalization of same-sex marriage, since legalization of same-sex marriage will not result in equal rights for men and women in legal disputes related to these unions.

In the wake of the passage of California's Proposition 8, Gays and Lesbians are showing their true colors displaying great hate of heterosexuals and just about everything we do.

Saturday, November 15th [2008] marks a day of hateful community-organized demonstrations, and predictable violence as well. Already, we have seen an old lady with a Cross beaten, hateful slogans plastered all over Mormon Churches, police cars damaged, and queer advocates baiting people into physical altercations to make themselves look good.

Blacks know precisely why the queer marriage movement's demands are fatally disingenous. "It's not a civil rights issue, because as African-Americans we can't change the color of our skin," said pastor Edward Smith, who supported the ban on gay marriage. That is why 70% of California blacks voted for Proposition 8.

The language of queer marriage movement is as shifty as the Arabic sands. They claim homosexuality is purely genetic, but elsewhere preen young people to "choose" being a homosexual. They want to inculcate kindergarteners by taking them on school field trips to witness lesbian marriages. They say they want "gay marriage," but litigate strenuously for laws that let any two human beings marry regardless of sexual orientation.

The queer marriage movement is indeed a hate movement targeting everything heterosexual. We are known as "breeders." Marilyn French, an advisor to Al Gore's presidential campaign, believes that "All men are rapists and that's all they are." Former Congresswoman Barbara Jordan insisted, "I believe that women have a capacity for understanding and compassion which man structurally does not have, does not have it because he cannot have it. He's just incapable of it." Gloria Steinem (who was sidelined by feminists for not being radical enough) believed that "The end of the institution of marriage is a necessary condition for the liberation of women."

Why do feminist leaders, who for forty years have erupted rivers of hate for marriage and husbands, now desperately want the entire socioeconomic institution of marriage for themselves? Why are they so hateful in their protesting to encourage the California Supreme Court to block Proposition 8?

In the January, 1988 issue of the N.O.W. [National Organization for Women] Times, radical feminist oracle Sheila Cronan had a featured inset that speaks volumes: *"The simple fact is that every woman must be willing to be **identified** as a lesbian to be fully feminist."* At the 1988 N.O.W convention in

Houston, Cronin declared; "Since marriage constitutes slavery for women, it is clear that the women's movement must concentrate on attacking this institution. Freedom for women cannot be won without the abolition of marriage."

Why would N.O.W. expect all women to pretend they are lesbians and fully devote themselves towards achieving a goal that only a few lesbians want? Why would N.O.W litigate vociferously for gay men while continuing to do everything possible to destroy the social rights of heterosexual men?

It is astonishing that gay men imagine N.O.W. is really working for them.

"Heather has two mommies" explains it all. It is a feminist vision for taking over the **economic** institution of marriage and the **social** institution of family (men cannot be parents outside marriage, unless they go to great lengths to adopt). Billions in federal social entitlement seed money is already available to feminists to buy out the marriage market, beginning with $16-billion in TANF [Temporary Assistance for Needy Families] block grants to states every year. This is why two-thirds of same-sex marriages in Massachusetts involve women—whose sexual preference is unknown.

N.O.W. cares nothing about gay men. It is using them as political fools to make SSM [same-sex marriage] appear "gender neutral." Gay men would receive little out of marriage. For them, marriage is largely an illusion masking a treatable and healable sexual disorder that is often disabling or fatal: gay men have 800% more sexual partners than heterosexual men. Like hetero men, gay men will be sucked dry for child support, but more stiffly be denied parental rights because they are gay.

It is astonishing that gay men imagine N.O.W. is really working for them. Heterosexual men thought the feminist equal rights movement (since the 1970's) stood for equality, and strongly supported it, until they found out personally what it means via a bankrupting surprise divorce or impossible child support order.

Indeed, same-sex marriage would result in severe societal stratification. It would place dual-female marriages-of-socioeconomic-convenience at the top of the socioeconopolitical diaspora, heterosexual marriages in the middle, and gay men at the very bottom.

In 1970, noted feminist author Shulamith Firestone issued a firebrand call predicting the demise of heterosexual marriage and the subsequent rise of the feminist same-sex marriage movement we see today:

> "The nuclear family is the school of values in a sexist, sexually repressed society . . . The alternative to the nuclear family at the moment is the extended family or the tribe. The growth of tribe is part of the process of destroying particularized roles and fixed erotic identity. As people develop fluid androgynous identity, they will also develop the forms of community appropriate to it. We cannot really imagine what those forms will be."

Now, I turn the tables on feminists, proving that what they want cannot be a Constitutional right:

> *"Heterosexual marriage is the only institution that fully and naturally erases all physical, economic, social, elective, legally-imposed, and culturally-imposed differences that exist between women and men. It is the only institution that harnesses the entire human race to work hard together and raise children in prosocial manner. It is the only institution that naturally assures everyone equal rights of every description regardless of race, sex, or creed. It is the whole cloth establishing one cooperative human race. Same-sex marriage cannot be constitutional because it would be the antithesis of equality structurally magnifying every tangible difference and disparity that exists between women and men, segregating marriages into at least three obviously dissimilar classes (female-female, hetero-*

sexual, and male-male), each with substantively different so-
cial, economic, and legal rights at law and public policy."

This declaration of fact is easily proven by first pointing
out that *Roe v. Wade* gives women exclusive control over re-
production and surrounding decisions. This precedent immediately translates into a strong or unilateral presumption as-
signing females custody of children, together with the social
institution of family and the rights, privileges, protections,
and social welfare benefits thereto; even in the elective absence
of marriage. The list of downstream family law statistical cita-
tions proving how the sexes are treated vastly differently, on
the basis of sex alone, is nearly endless and manifestly evident
in all aspects of family law and social policy.

Same-sex marriages are therefore not equivalent or simi-
larly situated for the purpose of asserting an equal rights
claim of action. . . .

Where the sexes are unquestionably treated differently before law in all these matters, an elective marriage between two
women and another elective marriage between two men would
facially enjoy vastly dissimilar rights, benefits, and protections.
Both would be unreasonably burdened with tremendously different responsibilities and sanctions before the law, regardless
of sexual orientation of participants in elective gender-
segregated marriages.

Where women have automatic control of children absent
marriage, and would have chattel ownership of children borne
into *elective* same-sex marriages, men's ability to be parents
and to participate in the very fabric of society would be fully
abrogated; while men would be required to economically support feminist marriages via an arrangement not dissimilar to
indentured servitude.

Same-sex marriages are therefore not equivalent or simi-
larly situated for the purpose of asserting an equal rights

claim of action on which high courts could justify issuance of broad orders forcing states to perform or recognize "same-sex marriage." Rather, the above analysis suggests that courts must ban same-sex marriage, on its face, to protect fundamental constitutional equal rights of men and women.

Feminists are now demanding courts seize control of marriage itself, at the complete disenfranchisement of Church.

George Washington was married without a state marriage license, as was everyone else back then. The Constitution was written intending for Churches to have exclusive control of marriage—protected as a fundamental right. Marriage did not fall under the purvue of the state in any way. In the mid 1800's some states began *requiring* marriage licenses for inter-racial marriages as a way to track miscegenation and discourage the practice. In 1923, the federal government enacted the Uniform Marriage and Divorce Act. By 1929, all states required marriage licenses.

Courts have dramatically seized incremental powers over marriage for states and trial lawyers to gratuitously manipulate, initially by giving the state sole control over divorce. With the passage of time, the notion of the separation between church and state has far exceeded its original dubious intent, and it being abused as a predatory devise. Feminists are now demanding courts seize control of marriage itself, at the complete disenfranchisement of Church.

Feminists have nearly fooled America into handing the institution of marriage over to them lock, stock, and barrel. The impact of this would be additionally as devastating to America as the feminist-inspired divorce and entitled-illegitimacy revolutions were.

Few thought that the divorce revolution would have a major impact on society or government. We now know that the impact has devastated state and federal budgets, created two generations of impoverished women and children, and a nation of disaffected men living on the fringes of society who cannot be responsible for their families because they are arbitrarily denied the fundamental right to be husbands and fathers. Many are brought up with no social proscript other than "getting by," playing video games, virtual relationships, and "shacking up."

Politicians have the audacity to call them "deadbeat dads," while mainstream television portrays them as idiots and jerks. I cannot imagine how it is possible for most boys to become mature, healthy adults in this contemporary diaspora. Images are powerful. Discrimination against boys in public education and the substituting of Ritalin for proper recreation and education is widespread. Boys brought up rarely seeing positive futures for themselves, while drugged with speed in school, will likely become intergenerational reflections of their massively abusive upbringing, with downward pressures on future generations.

We must recognize now that, if permitted, same sex marriage will become commonplace within two generations, causing serious compound socioeconomic problems. No large country has survived for long absent a strong institution of heterosexual marriage. Rome and the former U.S.S.R. are two primary examples that went morally, and subsequently economically bankrupt.

We cannot afford to roll over when barraged with terroristic admonitions uttered by hateful feminists. We will stand our ground. We will not sit on our thumbs or back down. Let us talk about it directly and factually. Let feminists isolate themselves as the radicals they truly are. Let us show them the door, as they walk their own gangplank right into the Pacific Ocean.

10

Supporting Gay "Couples" Restricts Resources Available to Families

National Observer Staff

National Observer *is a quarterly current events and politics magazine based in Melbourne, Australia.*

The decriminalization of sodomy has swung legislation in favor of homosexual lobby groups. "Anti-discrimination" laws compel employers to hire homosexuals, infringing upon freedom of association. In addition, politicians have given in to the pressure of endorsing "civil partnerships," which have been criticized by religious leaders. Emboldened by their successes, the aggressive homosexual lobby now seeks the recognition of "homosexual" marriages and its financial advantages. However, homosexual pairings are sexually unproductive and based on perverse acts. Subsidizing these groups with pensions, income tax concessions, and other benefits diverts support from conventional families, the basic unit of society.

It is now generally accepted that homosexual acts should not be criminally punishable if between adults. There are various arguments for and against this relaxation of the law. On the one hand it is argued that private acts between adults should not be subject to legal proscription; on the other hand it is argued that homosexual acts are a serious sexual perversion and should not be permitted by the law, even if actual prosecutions are rarely instituted.

It is after all apposite to note that homosexual activity (essentially sodomy) involves using the anus (an aperture for the emission of faeces) as an opening for the entry of another person's penis, the penis being of course an organ of procreation. This is regarded by many as a perversion, and it is easy to sympathise with that view. The abnormality of homosexuality is also evidenced by the indiscriminate multiple couplings—often extending into the hundreds or even thousands—to which homosexuals are prone. The homosexual lobby sets out to draw attention away from this phenomenon by referring instead to the relatively small number of "permanent" couplings.

However at all events it appears that the legalisation of homosexual acts has given rise to an extreme swing of the pendulum in favour of homosexuals. Homosexual lobby groups have been formed, under such names as the Victorian Gay and Lesbian Rights Committee. These groups have set out to achieve a position in which homosexual pairings have the same rights as conventional families. Up to the present time they have unfortunately had many successes, and it is time that their influence be reduced.

When Should Freedom of Association Be Abrogated?

One of the first objectives of the homosexual lobby was to prevent "discrimination" against homosexuals. This has been achieved to a large degree by "anti-discrimination" legislation. Typically this legislation makes illegal any discrimination against a homosexual in, for example, the context of job applications. Thus an employer who, understandably, regards homosexuals as perverted and does not wish to employ one may nonetheless be compelled by law to employ a homosexual.

It must be doubted whether this is a just position. Freedom of association properly means that persons should be able to select those with whom they associate. If, for any reason, one person does not wish to employ another, or does not wish to be employed by another, why should his wishes be overborne by the law?

However the legal compulsion to enter into contractual relationships with homosexuals is commonly part of a wider legislation scheme under which one may be compelled against one's will to enter into contractual relationships with others of a particular religion or racial group. Again, this compulsion is unjustifiable and inappropriate.

Pressure for homosexual "marriages" has arisen in the United States, England, Canada and Australia.

However there are other respects in which homosexual lobby groups attempt to go much further than the abrogation of contractual rights and of freedom of association.

Homosexual "Marriages"

An important matter on the agenda of the homosexual lobby is the recognition of homosexual "marriages" and the placing of these marriages on a par with true marriages.

Pressure for homosexual "marriages" has arisen in the United States, England, Canada and Australia. Recently Mr. Tony Blair, the [former] British Prime Minister, was reported as endorsing "civil partnership" laws to give homosexuals the same legal rights as married couples.

These proposals have been criticised by the Vatican.

In August 2003 a statement was issued, in the name of Cardinal [and current Pope] Joseph Ratzinger, [then] the Pope's principal theological adviser, and endorsed by the Pope himself. It stated inter alia:

> Those who would move from tolerance to the legitimisation
> of specific rights for cohabiting homosexual persons need to

be reminded that approval or legislation of evil is something far different from the toleration of evil.

There are absolutely no grounds for considering homosexual unions to be in any way similar or analogous to God's plan for marriage and family. Marriage is holy, while homosexual acts go against the natural moral law.

The Vatican statement went on to advise against laws authorising homosexual marriages:

To vote in favour of a law so harmful to the common good is gravely immoral.

There will of course be some who would seek to dismiss the Vatican statement on the basis that it represents a conservative approach. But it would be wrong to do this. Disapproval of homosexuality, which is widely regarded (and correctly so) as a perversion, flows through all sections of society, where there is particular concern at attempts by homosexuals to initiate sodomy with children and also with young men whose sexual orientation is not yet established. It is significant that homosexual lobbies have expended much energy in seeking the reduction of the age of consent for homosexual acts from eighteen years to sixteen years.

The aggressiveness of homosexual lobbyists is exemplified by threats by one Rodney Croome, a spokesman for the Tasmanian Gay and Lesbian Rights Group, who stated that distri bution of or quotation from the Vatican statement constituted a criminal offence. It was, he alleged, in breach of the State's anti-discrimination laws, since for example it referred to homosexuality as "deviant behaviour". (It is hard to see why sodomy should not be regarded as deviant behaviour.) And one David McCarthy, the president of the Victorian Gay and Lesbian Rights Lobby, said that the statement of the Catholic Church "could well be sedition", a claim which was of course absurd.

The encouragement of homosexuality was taken to new levels when in August 2003 Relationships Australia, a government-funded organisation for relationship counseling, "encouraged older women to explore lesbian relationships, which were seen as more nurturing and emotionally supportive".

Homosexual Activism in the High Court and in Parliament

Unfortunately an extreme homosexual activist—[Australian] Justice Michael Kirby—has been appointed to the High Court. Kirby speaks frequently in favour of homosexual activity. Indeed, in 2000 he addressed a meeting of students and others at St Ignatius' College, Riverview, in Sydney, and arguing in favour of homosexuality he asserted: "In my experience, few if any gay and lesbian people choose their sexuality. It is like your gender, your skin colour or being left-handed. From earliest days of puberty, you just know that is how you are. And if that is how you know you are, that is how God meant you to be."

One of the main purposes of the homosexual lobbies is to obtain for homosexual "couples" the same privileges as married people in regard to superannuation, pensions, and other financial advantages.

That statement by Justice Kirby was dishonest. Kirby well knew that puberty is a time of sexual confusion for many adolescents. Many adolescents have homosexual incidents, or experience transitory sexual desires with members of their own sex. However subsequently a large proportion of such adolescents settle down to normal heterosexual activity and marry or have long term relationships with members of their own sex. Only a minority become deviants.

It was indeed particularly unfortunate that it was at a school that Kirby made these regrettable statements. Did the parents of the students present know that their children would be exposed to homosexual propaganda and to an assertion that "from the earliest days of puberty" you know "how you are"? School children are particularly vulnerable to misinformation, especially from sources with respectable trappings (and especially justices of the High Court). And presumably there was no balancing statement from a speaker presenting the orthodox view that homosexual behaviour is an aberration that should be avoided.

Kirby's falsity exemplifies the undesirability of appointing homosexual activists, or persons who wish to persuade others of the propriety of homosexuality, to the High Court or to other judicial office. It appears that often such propagandists cannot restrain themselves, but in order to promote their cause make misleading statements.

Superannuation and Pension Rights

One of the main purposes of the homosexual lobbies is to obtain for homosexual "couples" the same privileges as married people in regard to superannuation, pensions and other financial advantages.

For example, it is often provided in pension plans that when a pensioner dies, his spouse succeeds to a pension, at a diminished rate. (This is the case, for example, for many pensions paid by Commonwealth and State governments to their retired employees. On the eventual death of the employee, a surviving spouse succeeds to the pension, at a reduced rate.)

The reason for permitting spouses to succeed to pension rights is the encouragement of the family. It has always been regarded—and properly so—as in the public interest that the family should be strengthened and supported, to encourage marriage and the rearing of children.

The family unit is basic to Western society, and also to all other societies. There must be recognition of the fact that where there is a marriage, commonly one of the parties must stay at home for at least part of the growing-up period of the children, and that the family will therefore suffer financially.

Families are accordingly given privileged treatment, not only in regard to many pensions, but also in regard to taxation. There are income tax concessions in favour of family groups, again for the purpose of encouraging and supporting the bringing up of children.

Homosexual groups do not have the requirements for financial support that families—the cornerstone of society—do.

But homosexuals fall completely outside this area of support. Homosexuals do not contribute children to society. In terms of producing future generations they are entirely unproductive. Their cohabitation or sexual conduct is based, not on the production of children, but indulgence in acts of anal sex or other perversions.

Accordingly there are no policy reasons in favour of providing financial subsidies to homosexuals. Indeed, to do so would be contrary to the interests of society, since there is a limit to the amount of funds available to assist individuals. By subsidising homosexuals less money would be available for proper purposes, such as supporting families.

Why Should Homosexuals Be Subsidised?

The foregoing demonstrates that there are compelling policy reasons not to subsidise homosexuals. Homosexual groups do not have the requirements for financial support that families—the cornerstone of society—do.

Politicians who, out of weakness, give way to demands of the homosexual lobbies are not fulfilling their duty. These demands are not well based, and politicians and others in positions of authority have an obligation to look to the interests of society as a whole.

11

Greater Acceptance and Support Helps Gay Families

Jane E. Brody

Jane E. Brody is the Personal Health columnist for the New York Times.

Over the past two decades, eroding homophobic attitudes and advances in reproductive technology have given rise to gay families. Growing up homosexual, many of these gays and lesbians— who never imagined they would have children—now adopt or choose artificial insemination or surrogacy. Also, most relatives of gay and lesbian parents come to embrace these growing families. Still, these households still face a lack of public and institutional support, despite clear evidence that children with gay and lesbian parents are as nurtured and well-adjusted as those raised by heterosexual couples.

Keith Lee Grant and Daniel Tamulonis had been partners for 15 years when Mr. Grant decided their self-focused life was too empty—that they had much more to give.

So eight years ago this interracial New York couple adopted a 2-day-old infant from Arkansas whom they named Isaac. Both dads quickly became adept at diaper changing, middle-of-the-night feeding and all the other challenges of child care.

Five years later, when life with Isaac settled into a manageable rhythm and the men were approaching 50, the cut-off age for adoptive parents, they adopted 3-day-old Trish.

Mr. Grant knew all along that he wanted children and had initially thought they would become foster parents. But Mr. Tamulonis said of the adoptions that have proved so rewarding: "We never looked back. I have Keith to thank for this. Having grown up gay, I never thought I would have a child in my life."

Linda and her partner Vicki had been together in Brooklyn for five years when they decided to start a family. Though Vicki wanted children but had no desire to bear one, Linda actively looked forward to pregnancy.

They decided on artificial insemination with sperm donated by a mutual friend. Since then, Linda bore first a girl and then a boy, who now have two mommies as well as a papa who sees them about once a month.

Along with advances in reproductive alternatives, the gradual erosion of homophobia over the past 10 or 15 years—a trend conspicuously on display last week in the Supreme Court's decision striking down a Texas sodomy law—has led to a sharp rise in the last 10 or 15 years in the number of openly gay men and women who have chosen to be parents.

According to the authors of *The Gay Baby Boom: The Psychology of Gay Parenthood* (New York University Press, $16.95) as many as 14 million children in the United States are being raised by at least one parent who is a gay man or lesbian.

Many are lesbian couples with children from earlier heterosexual marriages. But more and more gay couples are acquiring their own, through artificial insemination, adoption and, for some gay men, through a surrogate mother inseminated with their sperm.

The authors of *The Gay Baby Boom*, Dr. Suzanne M. Johnson and Dr. Elizabeth O'Connor, psychologists and life partners who are co-parents of two girls, decided to explore how families headed by lesbians and gay men come about and how well they are faring.

In 1999 and 2000 they conducted the largest national assessment of families headed by gay people who chose to participate. Data were collected from 415 parents—336 lesbian mothers and 79 gay fathers—living with their minor children in 34 states and the District of Columbia.

Succeeding as Gay Parents

Scores of earlier studies have already shown that on virtually every level of psychological adjustment—including peer relationships, gender development, intelligence, school performance and sexual orientation—children raised by gay parents are not significantly different from those raised by straight parents.

"How the children turn out depends on how you parent, not your sexual orientation," Dr. Johnson said in an interview. Parenthood requires unconditional love, respect, patience, consistent but appropriate discipline, along with actions and words that build a child's self-esteem, confidence and respect for individual differences. These qualities are not the sole province of heterosexuals, she said.

In fact, the study with Dr. O'Connor revealed that if anything, gay parents might do better, having gone to considerable trouble to become parents and being determined to raise children who respect themselves and others while remaining tolerant of diversity. An important goal of the parents was to instill a strong moral code in their children.

Furthermore, she added: "The sexual orientation of the parents seems to have no effect on the child's sexual orientation. The percentage of children raised by gay parents who turn out gay is no higher than that among children raised by straight parents."

Nor is the percentage of couples who break up after creating a family any higher among gays than among heterosexual couples, said Dr. Johnson, who is an associate professor of psychology at Dowling College in Oakdale, New York.

Dr. Johnson and Dr. O'Connor have been together for 19 years, deciding after 10 years to have their first child.

Ultimately most family members, including many with initial reservations about gays as parents, were delighted to become grandparents, aunts and uncles.

Although Linda and Vicki split up and Vicki moved out three months after their second child's birth, Vicki remains very much in their lives. As their noncustodial parent, she sees the children twice a week and contributes to their support.

Nearly half the lesbians and a quarter of the gay men in the survey experienced initial family disapproval about their decision to have children. A main concern, among family members as well as the couples, was whether the children would be subject to teasing and ostracism because their parents were gay.

But ultimately most family members, including many with initial reservations about gays as parents, were delighted to become grandparents, aunts and uncles.

As one respondent put it: "Initially, both sets of parents were less than thrilled with the idea. Once they realized I was serious, they softened a little. And once the baby was born, they were in love with her!"

Another reported that one brother-in-law had some reservations. "However, he read some research on children raised in gay families on the Internet and reversed himself," the authors reported.

Still, they concluded, there is by no means universal acceptance of these parents or their families.

Support and Opposition

"Lack of support from people and institutions outside the family is something that many gay and lesbian parents must face," the authors said. "Their approach to the outside world seems to be to present themselves as a family deserving of recognition and respect."

In completing school and camp applications in enlightened New York, Mr. Grant and Mr. Tamulonis have found that forms no longer ask for the names of mother and father but rather parent and parent. But three states—Florida, Mississippi and Utah—prohibit adoptions by gays.

As a group, the survey found, "gay- and lesbian-headed families scored as well as, or better than, heterosexual couples on measures of relationship adjustment and satisfaction, allocation of tasks related to child-rearing and housekeeping, and communication about their children."

All in all, the authors concluded, "our study and many other studies that have been done on gay- and lesbian-headed families show that gay men and lesbians make very effective parents."

The studies, they continued, show "strengths in the security of attachment to their children; in their parenting styles, including how they discipline their children; in the quality of their own couple relationships; and in how they share the work associated with raising children and running a household."

Perhaps many heterosexual couples with children and less than harmonious households could learn something.

Organizations to Contact

The editors have compiled the following list of organizations concerned with the issues debated in this book. The descriptions are derived from materials provided by the organizations. All have publications or information available for interested readers. The list was compiled on the date of publication of the present volume; the information provided here may change. Be aware that many organizations take several weeks or longer to respond to inquiries, so allow as much time as possible.

American Civil Liberties Union (ACLU)
125 Broad St., 18th Floor, New York, NY   10004
(212) 549-2500
Web site: www.aclu.org

The ACLU is the nation's oldest and largest civil liberties organization. Its Lesbian and Gay Rights/AIDS Project, started in 1986, handles litigation, education, and public policy work on behalf of gays and lesbians. The ACLU publishes the papers "Too High a Price: A Case Against Restricting Gay Parents" and "Working in the Shadows: Ending Employment Discrimination for LGBT [Lesbian, Gay, Bisexual, and Transgender] Americans" as well as an online newsletter, *ACLU Online*.

Children of Gays and Lesbians Everywhere (COLAGE)
150 Bryant St., Suite 830, San Francisco, CA   94103
(415) 861-5437 • fax: (415) 255-8345
e-mail: colage@colage.org
Web site: www.colage.org

COLAGE is a national and international organization that supports young people with lesbian, gay, bisexual, and transgender (LGBT) parents. Their mission is to foster the growth of daughters and sons of LGBT parents by providing education, support, and community. Their publications include the resource sheets *Tips for Making Classrooms Safer for Students With LGBT Parents* and *Tips for Coming Out to Your Kids*.

Concerned Women for America (CWFA)

1015 15th St. NW, Ste. 1100, Washington, DC   20005
(202) 488-7000 • fax: (202) 488-0806
e-mail: mail@cwfa.org
Web site: www.cwfa.org

CWFA is an educational and legal defense foundation that seeks to strengthen the traditional family by promoting Judeo-Christian moral standards. It opposes gay marriage and the granting of additional civil rights protections to gays and lesbians. CWFA publishes the monthly magazine *Family Voice* and various position papers on gay marriage and other issues.

Family Research Council (FRC)

801 G St. NW, Washington, DC   20005
(202) 393-2100 • fax: (202) 393-2134
Web site: www.frc.org

The council is a research, resource, and educational organization that promotes the traditional family, which the council defines as a group of people bound by marriage, blood, or adoption. The council opposes gay marriage and adoption rights. It publishes numerous reports from a conservative perspective on issues affecting the family, including homosexuality. FRC also hosts a weekly radio show, *Washington WatchRadio*.

Focus on the Family

Colorado Springs, CO   80920
(800) 232-6459 (A-FAMILY) • Fax: (719) 531-5181
Web site: www.focusonthefamily.org

Focus on the Family is a conservative Christian organization that promotes traditional family values and gender roles. Its publications include the monthly magazine *Focus on the Family* and articles regarding gender identity politics, homosexual rights and lifestyles, and the pro-gay Christian movement.

Human Rights Campaign (HRC)
1640 Rhode Island Ave., Washington, DC   20036-3276
(202) 628-4160 • fax: (202) 347-5323
Web site: www.hrc.org

The HRC provides information on national political issues affecting lesbian, gay, bisexual, and transgender Americans. It offers resources to educate congressional leaders and the public on such critical issues as ending workplace discrimination, combating hate crimes, fighting HIV/AIDS, protecting gay and lesbian families, and working for better lesbian health. HRC publishes *Equality* and *LAWbriefs*.

Lambda Legal Defense and Education Fund
120 Wall St., Ste. 1500, New York, NY   10005
(212) 809-8585 • fax: (212) 809-0055
Web site: www.lambdalegal.org

Lambda is a public-interest law firm committed to achieving full recognition of the civil rights of lesbians, gay men, and people with HIV/AIDS. The firm addresses a variety of areas, including equal marriage rights, the military, parenting and relationship issues, and domestic-partner benefits. It publishes the online newsletters *eNews* and *Of Counsel*.

Parents, Families & Friends of Lesbians & Gays (PFLAG)
1726 M St. NW, Ste. 400, Washington, DC   20036
(202) 467-8180 • fax: (202) 467-8194
Web site: http://community.pflag.org

A non-profit organization with over 200,000 members and supporters, PFLAG aims to promote the health and well-being of gay, lesbian, bisexual, and transgender persons, their families, and friends through support, education, and advocacy. It operates over 500 chapters in all 50 states.

REAL Women of Canada
Box 8813, Station T, Ottawa, ON
  K1G 3J1 Canada

(613) 236-4001 • fax: (613) 236-7203
e-mail: info@realwomenca.com
Web site: www.realwomenca.com

REAL Women of Canada (Realistic, Equal, Active, for Life) is a non-partisan, non-denominational organization of independent women in Canada that was federally incorporated in 1983. It publishes position papers upholding family values, traditional marriage, and views against same-sex unions as well its newsletter, *REALity*, which is issued six times a year.

Bibliography

Books

John Boswell — *Christianity, Social Tolerance, and Homosexuality: Gay People in Western Europe from the Beginning of the Christian Era to the Fourteenth Century.* Chicago, IL: The University of Chicago Press, 2005.

Joe Dallas — *The Gay Gospel?* Eugene, OR: Harvest House Publishers, 2007.

Francis MacNutt — *Can Homosexuality Be Healed?* Grand Rapids, MI: Chosen Books, 2006.

Gerald P. Mallon — *Lesbian and Gay Foster and Adoptive Parents: Recruiting, Assessing, and Supporting an Untapped Resource for Children and Youth.* Washington, DC: Child Welfare League of America, 2006.

Jonathan Rauch — *Gay Marriage: Why It Is Good for Gays, Good for Straights, and Good for America.* New York: Times Books/Henry Holt and Co., 2004.

Jack Rogers — *Jesus, the Bible, and Homosexuality: Explode the Myths, Heal the Church.* Louisville, KY: Westminster John Knox Press, 2006.

Ritch C. Savin-Williams — *The New Gay Teenager.* Cambridge, MA: Harvard University Press, 2005.

Glenn T. Stanton and Bill Maier	*Marriage on Trial: The Case Against Same-Sex Marriage and Parenting.* Downers Grove, IL: InterVarsity Press, 2004.
Andrew Sullivan, ed.	*Same-Sex Marriage: Pro and Con: A Reader.* New York, Vintage Books, 2004.

Periodicals

Gary Bauer	"The Aftershocks of Gay Marriage," *Human Events,* May 30, 2008.
David Blankenhorn	"Defining Marriage Down . . . Is No Way to Save It," *Weekly Standard,* April 2, 2007.
Mackenzie Carpenter	"What Happens to Kids Raised by Gay Parents?" *Pittsburgh Post-Gazette,* June 10, 2007.
Christian Examiner	"The Impact of Same-Sex Marriage on Religious Freedom," December 1, 2008.
Robert Epstein	"Same-Sex Marriage Is Too Limiting," *Los Angeles Times,* December 4, 2008.
Tyche Hendriks	"Same-Sex Couples Raising Children Less Likely to Be White, Wealthy," *San Francisco Chronicle,* October 31, 2007.
Jeff Jacoby	"Pregnant, Yes—But Not a Man," *Boston Globe,* April 13, 2008.

David J. Jefferson   "How Getting Married Made Me an Activist," *Newsweek*, November 24, 2008.

James Kirchick   "Golden Opportunity: How the GOP Helped Bring Gay Marriage to California," *The Advocate*, August 12, 2008.

Jennifer Roback Morse   "Winning Proposition," *National Review*, November 6, 2008.

David Muskera   "A Gay Adoption Head Scratcher," *American Chronicle*, May 14, 2008.

Julia Reischel   "See Dick Be Jane," *Broward-Palm Beach New Times*, May 18, 2006.

Thomas Rogers   "What the Pregnant Man Didn't Deliver," *Salon*, July 3, 2008.

Time   "The Battle Over Gay Teenagers," October 2, 2005.

Jesse Washington   "Is Gay the New Black? Marriage Ban Spurs Debate," *Associated Press*, November 30, 2008.

WorldNetDaily   "Homosexual Adoption Report Written by 'Pro Gay Advocate,'" March 25, 2006.

Index

A

Abortion activism (1973), 15
Acceptance
    of gay families, 87–91
    of gay marriage, by society,
        12, 15
    by parents, of gay children,
        28, 52–59, 60–68
ACLU (American Civil Liberties
    Union), 23, 38–39
Adolescence (journal), 20
Adoption by gay couples
    family values, 42–43
    Florida's banning of, 29, 44
    gay baby boom, 35–36
    "Lawrence Effect," 37
    marriage factor, 36–37
    molestation by gay men,
        37–38
    second-parent trap, 40–42
    state efforts at banning, 45
    states in favor of, 33
    Tasker-Golombok study, 45,
        46
    See also Florida; National
        Council on Adoption;
        Second-parent adoption
        policy
Adoption Nation (Pertman), 39
*Adults Raised as Children in Les-
    bian Families* (report), 46
The Advocate (journal), 17, 19, 22
AgapePress (Christian news
    service), 34
AIDS/HIV, 5, 14, 17, 34, 60, 65, 66
Alliance for Marriage, 70–71

American Academy of Pediatrics,
    38
American Civil Liberties Union
    (ACLU), 23, 38–39
*American Journal of Diseases of
    Children*, 17
*American Journal of Orthopsychia-
    try*, 46
American Psychological Associa-
    tion, 26
American Sociological Review, 20,
    24, 46
Archives of Sexual Behavior
    (study), 20

B

Balkman, Thad, 41
Bauer, Allison, 40
Bazile, Leon, 72
Benne, Robert, 11–15
Biblarz, Timothy J., 24, 27, 29
Blair, Tony, 82
Blankenhorn, David, 8
Brody, Jane E., 86–91
Brown, Jerry, 7

C

California
    adoption data, 32
    Education Code, 7
    equal rights establishment,
        69–72
    harmfulness of gay marriage
        in, 73–79
    Proposition 8, 8–10, 73